# SERIOUSLY

# SIMPLE

# STUFF TO

# GET YOU

# UNSTUCK

# SERIOUSLY SIMPLE STUFF TO GET YOU UNSTUCK

**STRONGER BRAVER WISER**

Published by

Stronger, Braver, Wiser Publishing

www.strongerbraverwiser.com

*36 22 09*

SERIOUSLY SIMPLE STUFF TO GET YOU UNSTUCK

Copyright © 2016 by Tony Curl

Paperback ISBN -    978-0-9953649-0-5
Ebook ISBN -    978-0-9953649-1-2

Published by:

Stronger Braver Wiser Publishing
Think and Grow Business
SAN – 908-1089
Brisbane, Qld, Australia.
P: 1300 866 928
www.strongerbraverwiser.com


Cover Design – Chamillah Designs
www.chamillah.com

# Dedication

This book is dedicated to an incredible influence in our lives, Carter and two amazing parents Ashleigh and Jarade. The strength Carter showed in his short life, is a source of inspiration while the ongoing strength and caring nature of Ash and Jarade amaze and inspire those that know them.

Love to my wife Sharon, the founding president and driving force of Carter's Cause, the foundation for which this book benefits. A testimony for an amazing influence on us all.

Love to my beautiful wife, Sharon and two wonderful kids Tim and Tayla who have stood beside me on my journey.

## Praise for Seriously Simple

*"Do You Know Yourself? This book made me smile, made me curious, made me cry then took me back to my favourite days as a child. Make tomorrow today - Definitely a book to read to get unstuck."* - **Clare Sandy, Thought Leader. Brisbane, Qld.**

*"Seriously Simple Stuff is a tremendous example of what's really important in life. Personally, it took me away from the daily grind and reminded me of what's REALLY important - the basics we all take for granted most of the time. The other aspect the book conveyed to me, was the style through which the author himself communicates his message. I could actually hear the voice of Tony Curl ringing in my ears as I was reading this book. It's like having your very own coach in your living room! Seriously Simply Stuff is a seriously good read!"* – **Brad Tupper, Queensland Sales Manager, Brisbane, Qld.**

*I knew that Tony's book would be as inspirational as what he is, keeping me inspired by every page. As a manager, I always looked up to you and took every word you spoke to me onboard. Your advice and knowledge, so grounded and humble. Which is why your book, Simple Stuff, was such an amazing read. The kind of empowering book I could read over again. I could absorb all your wise words, to help impact in my own everyday life. Life that is amazing if you embrace it. Thank you Tony, for being the great motivator that you are and always have been and giving us this great book."* **Renee Cosh, @inspiringyouxo , Gold Coast, Qld**.

# Table of Contents

## STRONGER BRAVER WISER

# Foreword

When asked by Tony Curl to write the foreword to this book, I couldn't help but feel honored for a myriad of reasons. Highest among these was the idea that someone I consider of such high caliber would think such of me as to include me in this very personal endeavor of becoming a published author.

Tony is a great guy who, after three decades of success in the Retail Management world, committed himself to achieving higher education and venturing into Behavioral Coaching with the vision of helping people around the world achieve their greatest goals. His dedication to his family, his friends, and his skillset is admirable and I feel blessed to have the opening word in this beautiful collection of Tony's thoughts.

We could all use a little boost…

If I have learned anything, it's that life has a way of answering questions you didn't even ask.

This wonderfully challenging journey of life offers seemingly endless opportunities to grow, adapt, or remain stagnant. There are times we come upon such realizations on our own, while sometimes relying on the wisdom of others.

I am forever grateful to those, like Tony, who seek to inspire and empower others. With the many twists and turns of our journey, it is the empowered mind that reveals to us that sometimes we have to lose to win... that we are greater than what we've settled for, and that happiness and success are more than a feeling; they're a behavior.

Cheers to those much-needed souls who fan the flames of the empowered mind.

We've all been around long enough to realize that life can hit you hard! Suddenly, when you least expect it, WHAM; life has a knack for challenging you in ways that you don't feel prepared for. It's as if, in some comedic twist, life enjoys testing you in a manner in which you feel least equipped.

When this is happening, it's easy to drop into a victim mindset. It's easy to feel stuck, defeated, and like you are a losing player in the game of life. This victim mindset argues (very loudly) that we have lost; that nothing good is on the horizon. Never forget that the volume of an argument does not reflect the validity of the argument. Just because the victim mentality argues that we are losing, doesn't mean that it's true. In fact, I have come to realize that during the times in my life where I thought I was losing, I was actually winning.

Your agreement with reality defines your life… An empowered perspective helps us see that we can only get stronger when working against resistance. It is when we struggle that we strengthen. It is when challenged to our core that we learn the depth of who we are. It is when we feel broken that we can learn from our experiences and refine our own ability to mend ourselves and others.

Perhaps our greatest wisdom will reveal that it's the painful tears of our past that water the beautiful blossoming of our future. Maybe it's through the broken hearts that we receive the boost we need to appreciate the depth and magnificence of love. It's through this experiential journey of life that we are sure to go through all of the ups and downs, the wins and losses, the kindness, and betrayals; while finding ways to connect with happiness, love, and success.

Because of this, I am so grateful for people like Tony Curl; those who selflessly endeavor to help others. I'm honored to write the foreword to this first masterpiece. For me, Tony is sure to climb in his recognition as one of the greats; whose words will be repeated and shared for many years after initially spoken and written.

This book is a treasure chest of wisdom, experience, and insight. May it help you navigate through this journey of life and find inspiration as you connect with his brilliant mind. Tony is a friend to me; a friend to all of us. Enjoy!

Steve Maraboli
New York, USA

**Note from the Author.**

I am forever indebted to Dr. Steve Maraboli. I am humbled to know him and count him as a friend. His wisdom changes lives, challenges more and will go down in history as well ahead of existing thinking and science. His studious knowledge of human behaviour is changing the way we coach and influence others and his reach is global. I am honoured and incredible humbled for his support and mentorship and I am eternally grateful.

Tony Curl,
Brisbane, Australia

# Preface

*"Nothing changes until something moves" – Albert Einstein*

*STUCK - be fixed in a particular position or unable to move or be moved.*

Life is not meant to be easy. But it can be simple. Seriously simple in fact. You may be asking how this may be. There is no doubt that you're busy, there is no doubt that you have had effort. But the best of life continues to elude you.

We are partners in our own deception. The lies we tell ourselves. The life we have settled for, when we yearn for the life we wish for. We become our own worst enemy as we yearn for the things we don't have and discredit the gifts we have.

Life can be simple.

When I first started writing this book, I was challenged on the name. Challenged by my wife Sharon and my daughter, Tayla.

"What do you mean Seriously Simple?"

Let me explain. Life can be simple. We are the ones that complicate it. We are the ones that make it hard. We are the ones that make the excuses. We are the ones that miss the lessons in life. We are the ones that miss our gifts.

When we make some adjustments, we can really simplify our life. When we simplify we clarify and, in turn, purify.

That's what I mean by seriously simple. It can be simple, and by making life as simple as we can, we increase our chances for success.

"Ok, then, so what do you mean by Stuff?"

Stuff, relate back to stories, strategies and sayings. I have learnt that people don't respond well to being told what to do, but when "simple stuff" is presented, it stands a greater chance to resonate. We love stories, we love story telling. Stories bind us to life, they resonate within, they drive change.

So, I share "my stuff" with you in this book. And that seriously simple stuff can help you get unstuck. Take away the learning and make it work for you.

I know you will take away some simple stuff that will help you get you unstuck, the fact that you are also supporting "Carter's Cause Inc." with the purchase should make it mean even more.

Getting unstuck is one of the most common issues I hear from my clients. They get stuck in life, in relationships, in their careers, in their businesses, they get stuck with their feelings and emotions, they get stuck and can't seem to move forward.

We look for the magic formula. The magic formula to get ourselves unstuck, to get us moving forward. And that magic formula does exist, by reading through "my stuff", it will uncover itself to you.

**To you. The magic formula is uncovered by you.**

# Introduction

Life is simple.

So why do we complicate it?

We complicate it when we create complex ways to grow, lead and manage our lives. We are constantly faced with a barrage of media and marketing that continually tells us otherwise, a barrage designed to make us feel bad and to make us buy the very thing we need that will make us feel better. Our news programs tell us everything that is wrong in the world and only highlight the extreme examples of good inspiration because they are that far removed from the everyday. We chase the illusion of happiness by chasing a material world of success.

Heaven forbid if we actually believed we could have a great life.

Millions are spent every year on studies and research designed to unlock the secrets of highly successful leaders, and we clamour to spend our money on the latest sure-fire guaranteed method of success. Our business leaders search for the method to bring in the dollars, while many of us search for the best way to bring instant money. Online marketing, search engine optimisation, playing the stock markets…the list goes one.

Many confuse the simple life, with an easy life. Low maintenance homes are offered; estates are marketed for "making the most of your leisure time". Work-life balance is offered up by many companies as a means for their workforce. The idea of sitting on the beach drinking the latest fab drink is a symbol of how best to live life, but it's not based on reality. If that was indeed the norm, we would be led by a group of unbelievable alcoholics dying young from liver disease. At least, it would create career paths, I'm guessing.

Many confuse the simple life, with being average and flying under the radar. Far from it. Simplifying your life allows you to soar and gives you the best possible opportunity to reach the greatest version of you. To truly align your purpose, your passion and your potential. Living simply creates a focus and an awareness that will enable you, and empower you to achieve greater success than where you currently stand.

Here is the way I see it.

- Life is Life
- Life is Simple
- Life isn't easy
- Life is created by the choices we make
- Life is determined by our actions.

If you understand this, you'll go a long way to understanding the stories and methods in this book. Sharing my thoughts has been part of my journey and one that is backed by experience and the continued research of me, by me. I didn't collaborate with CEO's around the world, to verify my thoughts. I have real-life experiences that when I share, I add value.

This book is not for the following people.

- The Devil's Advocate. Those who believe that I am not living in the real world, will have a hard time understanding how to simplify their lives.
- Haters. We know them. The world is against us, so we will send our venom out to the world. They poison everything about themselves with the continued ability to spread their venom. Every time the spread hate, they further poison inside.
- Factions of Fact. Those that demand scientific evidence before they acknowledge the existence of any contrary thought.

I subscribe to the thought that it doesn't matter if it's right or wrong. What matters is what works. And does matters what works for you. FOR YOU. And I know this can work for you. I have cases upon cases where simplifying life brings greater success, greater satisfaction and a huge opportunity to bring significance to your life.

Do you want to read on and learn more? YES! There are some over-riding concepts you need to grasp before heading into the world of simplifying your life. These are:

1. Don't be an asshole.
2. Respect all things. (That means people, creatures, the world, the environment …get the picture)
3. Each story can stand singularly to gain better effect in your life.
4. Each story can be used in conjunction to gain even better effect in your life.
5. You choose how to make the stories work. Some you may choose to ignore; some you will see immediate benefit from an Ah-ha moment.

Each story has been written as a standalone simple story. If you are looking for a book that builds to a final WOW! This isn't it. Or it might be. Simple stories to support your journey to a simple life. Some stories will give the reader a similar message to a previous one.

We need people to think. We need people to think better. We need people to think more. Reflection is a valuable tool, but only in the way to drive a way forward. I personally find it almost humorous when the latest leadership study comes out. It is very rare to see one that my thoughts don't align to. I have aligned myself with two international experts in John Maxwell and Steve Maraboli, because in both cases their work, values and humility resonate with me and my thoughts. They also add value to many around the world, and also choose to acknowledge they cannot save everyone. Our perception of the world, is governed by how we think.

As you read this book, look for the messages and look for the challenges on how you think. So check your thoughts regularly, and keep them aligned with your desired thoughts.

If you challenge your thoughts, your perceptions this book will be the Seriously Simple thing that gets you UNSTUCK.

## The Past is Behind You

The past is the past. Simple. We call it the past, because it has passed you by. It's gone, it's been done, it's had its day It's done and dusted. If you are dragging yesterday into today, the reality is it is dragging you away from the joy of today.

It doesn't matter what happened yesterday; it doesn't matter what happened last week; it doesn't matter what happened ten years ago. It doesn't matter who you had a crush on in high school. It doesn't matter how you missed your high school football team. It doesn't matter about that time you embarrassed yourself in front of your family.

Nothing you do today can change any of that. Let me say that again. NOTHING you do today can change what happened in the past.

The past is our journey. The past is our history. The past is our learnings. The past is what has got us where we are today. Our actions, our adventures, our mis-adventures, our mistakes, our problems. They are the foundation of where we are today.

They are now who we are. Our past does not define us. We should learn from our past, and that's it. We all make mistakes.... all of us. Learn and move on.

In 2011, I was rocked to my very core with a mess that occurred in my life. I lost a lot of things close to me and because of the situation, lost some people close to me. I was shattered. Shattered. At the time I didn't see a way forward. I had all the coulda's and shoulda's in the world. How could this have happened to me? I didn't deserve this! I was wallowing in my own self-pity.

In the end, the only thing I could do was simple.

What happened, had happened. I couldn't look anywhere else but with me. What did I do to create the mess? What actions of mine had led to the series of events? How had I contributed to this?

I needed to realise my role in the drama and it was only then that I could learn and be better for it, and it was only then that I could move forward. I needed to move forward and had to look at each day as a way of becoming a better me. And when I got better, the people around me reciprocated.

My Mum had been battling cancer for some time and after this shattering event I was called to serve her in the time she had left. It was special, it was humbling. It was a time when my only concern was my mum's final wishes and my daily focus ensured this.

I still remember my last visit with her. It was a Friday afternoon. She was in her palliative care bed and her frail body was heaving with every breath. She was asleep, but far from peaceful. That afternoon I sat in her room just being there. Just being present. I had nowhere else I would rather be. Mum's wishes had been completed. And I just wanted to be there.

She woke briefly and sensed my presence. She asked me just one question after saying hello. The final wish had been to bring back my Father's ashes to Brisbane and complete the plans for Mum and Dad to be laid together.

"Is everything done?" "Yes, Mum," I replied with tears in my eyes. "Thank you."

A long pause took over as I sensed the realisation of what was happening. In time she asked if I was still there and what I would be doing the rest of the day. It was about 4pm in the afternoon. I had nowhere else to go, and let Mum know this and I would just stay with her for a while.

"Ok, I just need to go back to sleep" Mum said in a voice so low and strained that I struggled to hear. "That's ok Mum, I'll just stay for a little bit"

I left hours later, the vision of Mum's heaving chest as she struggled for breath in a fitful sleep firmly in my mind. Obviously we didn't have much time, but it still came as a shock when we got the call at 8am Saturday morning, while getting ready to come up and see Mum, that she had passed away.

There was sadness, of course. There was relief as Mum was no longer in pain and she could finally join Dad who had passed away in 1987.

I felt honour. I felt humble that I had been given this chance to serve my mum. I was humbled for those times we spent together.

I visit Mum and Dad's memorial site, whenever I need clarity. Whenever I need "me time". I'll sit and have a coffee and allow my thoughts to focus. Rarely does a day go by when I don't think of Mum and Dad, and it's a common scenario when people lose someone, they feel closer to them after death. Life has a habit of getting in the way, sometimes.

On reflection, I needed these two events, they happened for a reason.

They forced me to look internally at my behaviours and at my agenda. Being called to serve my Mum highlighted the need to bring out the real me, what was inside me. I realised I needed to change.

I could have been bitter! I could have been angry! Both events happened. I chose to look at what the lesson was and the learnings. Nothing I could do could change what happened. I created a mess and paid a cost for that, and my Mum passed away from cancer. I couldn't stop that. All I could do was to do what I did. Serve my Mum and fulfil her dying wishes and learn from the mess I created.

It was a clear choice. Focussing my energy on the positive learnings and service, allowed me to create a better me. Focussing my energy backwards, would have created a poison within me that eventually would have eaten me from in the inside out.

Around the world, many live in the past. Focussing their energy and emotions on things they cannot control, trying to understand and contemplate the reasoning behind events from the past.

We live for yesterday, we live for last week, we live for last year.

We believe in the good old days; we believe our best is in the past. Our past is our memories, our past is our learnings, our past should stay where it is. And we should let it.

I learnt to live in the present. To make the most of everyday. To continue to live and make the most of what I have and what I can deliver.

What happened has happened. Do the very best you can today. Stop thinking of all the Woulda's, Coulda's and Shoulda's from your past. These thoughts serve you no purpose and can lead to poisoning you.

Focus on what you can do today. And when you learn to think like this, your life does gets clearer, your life starts to get simpler.

**People who focus on making the best out of every day and making the right decisions and combining with the right actions, leads us on a path to living simply.**

## Simply Musing – Eyes Averted

My morning walk with Sharon, in the city we love and live in, Brisbane, Queensland. We usually walk by the water around our home suburbs, we venture to the city and other places on weekends to broaden our view of the world. It's different in the city. Walking along Southbank, across the bridges that straddle our river, I am feeling happy and fulfilled. Walking with the one I love, in a city I love, with a view to cherish puts me in a place of sharing my happiness and joy. Around our normal walks, a good morning, a good-day, a play with a dog, a smile a good nature chuckle are just par for the course. We share our smiles; we share our joy.

In the city it's different. More self-absorbed, more conscious, averting eye contact. I willingly looked for eye-contact when we were coming up to others and only a few responded. Eyes averted, engrossed in self. Understanding the world is what we make it, what we perceive it to be. I was filled with joy and was happy to share, bur felt unable to do so. Will it stop me in the future…HELL NO. Why are we so self-absorbed? Why are we so self-conscious? Accepting a smile from someone that wants to give it should brighten your day. Be happy with that thought, that someone felt enough care to share what was in their heart at the time. What are you looking for on the ground anyway? Lift your head, Ok pump your music up if need be, but share that experience with who you come into contact with. Try it, you might like it.

## STRONGER BRAVER WISER

*"Each day is filled with promise, potential and possibility."*

*"At some time you start to think your dreams are beyond you. The universe is sending you messages to quit... contrary. The universe is simply making sure that it really is something you want. Anything great is worth fighting for. Keep fighting, keep persisting. It is only through persistence that we ultimately succeed."*

*"Surround yourself with people who move you, motivate you and mobilize you."*

"Your view on the world is validated and verified daily. How is your view on the world working for you?"

"Getting defensive doesn't hide the fact that you know you could have done better. Stop putting your energy into your excuses."

"A well lived life means weathering a few storms. Our lessons don't come from sunny days on the beach, they come from copping a few waves on the head."

"I get it! Something painful happens and that hate flares within and sticks around. Hate keeps the pain; forgiveness let's it go. Hate breeds poison, forgiveness breeds peace. When you chain yourself to hate, you chain yourself to pain."

*"Always appreciate what is. Take the time and enjoy the world. It's not what you do, it's not what you have. It's what you become that is important. Strive to become more."*

*"I'm not going to tell you that life will get better. But I will say, magnificent rewards await those who keep forging ahead towards their dreams."*

*"Hope builds and creates dreams. Fear keep us firmly entrenched in the status quo."*

*"We are masters of excuses. Have you ever just acted on something and gained so much from it. Act with intention and you will be surprised at how well you can do."*

*"It doesn't matter where you are or what you do, it's only when we give up on our dreams do we really stop living. Don't give up."*

*"You get the results your belief dictates."*

## 4 Steps to a Simpler Life

We live hectic lives. We're busy. 24/7. We're overworked, and underappreciated. It just doesn't stop. Our jobs; career, family demands, friends and our community. The demands placed on us. The time pressures. We bounce from issue to issue, deadline to deadline, demand to demands. Our lives aren't ours and we are not in control. We become like the ball in a pinball arcade game, as we bounce around with the pressures

We yearn for the easy life. We're inundated from easy-life marketers", it's out there, it's available and their products are just what we need. And we feel bad because of it. We yearn for this easy life, but we are yearning for something that doesn't exist. Life wasn't meant to be easy, in fact it's often brutal. Realising that life wasn't meant to be easy or even fair, is the day we should start focusing on what we do have and what we do want.

Life isn't easy but it can be simple. Simplifying your life drives momentum and creates flow, and in doing so, a happier you.

### Step 1. Know what you want!

Sounds really simple, doesn't it? Often we don't know what we want.

We cannot articulate it. We do know what we don't want, "I don't want to be fat"; "I don't want a bad job"; "I don't want to have a bad day"; "I don't want to have my business fail". We verbalise our thoughts on what we don't want. And when we do this, the universe has the habit of delivering exactly what we don't want. We end up overweight, unhappy, unappreciated and unfulfilled.

We get what we focus on. So, focus on what you want! "I want to be healthy and fit": "I want to work for a great boss in a great job"; "My business will be successful"

We have multiple "I Wants". What do you want in your career, your family, your social circles, your spiritual and health aspects of your life? Having that clear understanding starts the process of living more simply.

AND, be specific. Ask people what they want and you will generally get answers like: Money, Fame, Win the Lottery etc. It is hard to motivate yourself when you have a general want, instead create a specific desire and watch the power behind that. Get specific on what you want and start the process of simplifying your life.

**Step 2. Understand what is important**.

What's helping you and what's hurting you? When people know what they want, they begin to understand what is important to them. They analyse what they have in their life and what they do and keep on track by asking simple questions.

- Is this helping me?
- Is this hurting me?

If it helps them, they continue doing it with increased focus, but if they determine it is hurting them, they let it go.

Ask yourself these questions next time you have time demands or facing distractions. If you answer them relative to the importance of what you are chasing, you will respond accordingly.

If it is helping you, keep it up. If it hurts you, stop.

**Step 3. Align your actions to what is important.**

This is the big step, and where most people will fail. It's now about putting action into place. If being happy at home is important, your actions need to align with that. If working towards a better job is important, your actions need to be in alignment. If you know what you want, and understand what is important but fail to do action, you will fail. Failing creates situations where we lose control of our agenda and breeds dissatisfaction.

People get stuck and the main cause is the lack of taking the required actions aligned to their goals. Align your actions to your goals and dreams. Get going, daily and every day. Don't wait another day waiting for someday or one day. Align your actions. Start today. Do it every day.

**Step 4. Maintain Clarity.**

Our final step is to keep these focused. At times life will still send you curly ones that are out of your control, so maintaining your clarity is vital. You can maintain clarity in simple ways, by having a vision board, or even just post-it notes on the bathroom mirror. Keeping focused stops you drifting back to old ways and bad habits. Clarity is king.

Following these steps will allow you to live your life that becomes simpler. They remove the needless drama, the toxic people and the bad situations because you realise they don't help you in achieving the life you want.

A beautiful sidenote is, once the toxins and dramas are removed, you purify your life. Simplify and purify. What better way to live your life? Simple and pure!

Give it a shot, what have you got to lose? When you simplify your life, you give yourself the best chance to achieving what you want.

STRONGER BRAVER WISER

# Choose a Good Autopilot!

Research continues to tell us what some of you may already know. We are on auto-pilot. The advancements in neuroscience shows that as self-aware primates we have very little control over our thoughts, actions and behaviours.

But that little, means a lot.

It is accepted that over 90% of our thoughts, actions and behaviours happen to us automatically. Our remote control kicks in, and we go on auto-pilot. Research tells us this covers 97% of our everyday actions. **Wow!**

Marketing now tells us that the decision to purchase happens milli-seconds before we become consciously aware of that decision. **What!** We have decided to buy! The decision was made before we were consciously aware of it. Just think about that. We believe we are making the choice, but really, are we?

Think also about others who do unspeakable acts after hearing voices in their heads. Does that mean, the voices happened prior to them being consciously aware of them. If we are truly creatures of automation, is anyone actually responsible for their own actions, thoughts and behaviours. The case majority of us are hard-wired and surely that absolves us of blame and responsibility. Doesn't it?

As I said, the little we do have control of, means a lot.

We are blessed with conscious thought. And even if our brain triggers decisions prior to us becoming conscious of it, the fact remains we soon become conscious of it and that is when we choose to either do its not to do it.

That is when the choice we make to have a good auto-pilot kicks in. While we may be hard-wired we can choose to rewire. By consciously choosing to do better actions, we can rewrite our neural pathways and create new habits and actions. We never erase our previous pathways, but we can strengthen the new ones, so that they do become part of our auto-pilot. We still have a choice and it's a choice to override our automatic choice.

And let us thank our spiritual leader (whoever that may be for you) for that. Instead of being slaves to our impulses, emotions and desires we can choose to be the masters of our own destiny.

What was that Tony, instead of being slaves to our impulses, emotions and desires we can choose to be the masters of our own destiny?

So why do I still feel a slave to my impulses, emotions and desires?

Many still are. Many are controlled by drug, self-induced or prescribed. Many react their way through life, becoming the victim of the first thing that comes out of their mouth, becoming the victim of remorse after an action or behaviour they seemingly had no control over. The sad fact is, many still are slaves to their impulses, emotions and desires.

And we have the tools. We have the tools to choose. They are free, and within you now! It is the tool of conscious thought. Imagine your life and how it could be better if you used the power of conscious thought effectively?

Because we do have the tools, sometimes I just want to shake people. People in that robotic, drone-like state, walking the earth with no set mission other than to survive another day. Missing the glory of the day, missing the potential for beauty and magic that each moment brings. Missing the gift of life, to walk in the footsteps of the mundane.

And you see them too! You may even feel like one at times, waking to the alarm clock, leaving your dreams to sleep, getting off to a job you don't like, bravely working with people you detest, all to be doing what you perceive your life is.

There is more to life. There is more to you. And that is where the choice of a good auto-pilot is critical. It instils in us the habits of success, the continual quest for growth, and the desire to chase our goals. Our auto-pilot is one of our own choosing. It understands that sometimes the temporary pain of earning a living in a job you don't like is needed, to put a roof over your head and food on the table. But it shouldn't derail you from the life you desire.

What life can you create when those activities spent "killing" or "wasting" time were put into the quest for a better you? What would your life be like if instead of "chilling and net flicks" you devoted time to wellness and thinking? A much better life awaits you with some simple choices, backed by intentional actions.

There will always be the stuff we do consciously. That will always be the stuff within our control. When better choices are backed with intentional action, we build the neural pathways needed to improve your auto-pilot. Focus on the controllable.

Slave or master? What is your choice? We live on auto-pilot. Isn't it time you made it a good one?

# STRONGER BRAVER WISER

## Simply Musing - Stop it. Please stop. Stop Apologising.

Stop it. Please stop. Stop apologising. I've heard it before. You apologise to others, you apologise to yourself. You apologise for being YOU. You are magnificent and have everything you need to have within you now. So stop apologising and get out and unleash your greatest potential for the world to see. You have a responsibility to the world. To bring out your best. To bring out everything that is awesome about you, and leave the apologising for others that don't get it. I know you get it and to really get it, you seriously just have to get out there and do it. Have a go, by having a go you are already in front of everyone else not having a go. Not giving the time and the energy to unlock and unleash their greatest self...but you can. So stop saying and being sorry and get out there and make YOU happen.

*"We need to simplify life. Do you think grass thinks about who trod on it yesterday? No... It just continues to grow. And so should you. You cannot control who treads on you, but you do control your own growth. Don't ever let others inhibit you!"*

*"Vulnerability brings honesty. We become most honest with ourselves when we are faced with real fear around a situation or an outcome. Yet many still stay in their comfort zone, listening to their own excuses and lies."*

*"People value people who value people."*

*"Have you inspired someone today by your actions?"*

*"Persistence separates those who want it more."*

*"Persistence to fight for what you want is what separates those who win and those who don't."*

*"It's only when you put action into practice will you ever really unlock the real possibilities that surround you."*

*"What in your life needs to be consigned to the bin? Just make sure it's not your dreams!"*

*"Your beliefs stimulate action. Actions drive results. Focused action creates success."*

*"We learn lessons and move on. Stop being haunted by yesterday. Learn and move on. That's what life is about. Today. Make the most of it."*

*"When you find yourself internally, you find what nourishes you from within. You lose that entitlement and anger when YOU deliver."*

*"Even small waves make it to shore. Use the potential you have through intention and action and enjoy your journey."*

"Your journey is successful if you have done the best with what you have."

"Are new mistakes the key to success? At least it's better than making the same mistakes."

"One thing that is guaranteed not to work. Doing Nothing. A goldmine when you realise it. Don't be paralysed by analysis. Don't be paralysed by fear. The one thing that is guaranteed not to work. Doing nothing achieves nothing."

"Great days ahead if you believe and if you act."

## Detach and Observe to Win the Battle

Every day we face an interesting battle. It's an internal battle. And it's a battle that has a winner every time. Whether that winner is good for us is another question, but every battle has a winner. Let's observe this battle and I will share a strategy that works for me.

Inside us we have our ingrained habits, wired into our brain for maximum effect. They operate within us and depending on the quality of our behaviours, these hard-wired habits are either good or bad for us. Because they are wired-in, they occur automatically.

It's a battle within when our habits contradict with the life we desire.

People ask me how long it takes to change a habit. Some experts provide the days needed to adapt a new habit to erase a bad habit. The challenge is, the bad habits still remain wired in. It hasn't been erased, just replaced and the danger remains that we may regress. This has been proven many times within the study of conditioning. Good habits replace bad habits, but bad habits can be refired when we regress.

I say good habits occur daily. It's a daily choice.

I have been getting up at 5am for the best part of the last seven years. This is my time that I spend with my wife, getting our morning walk in and getting our day off to the best possible start.

Yet.

Every morning, when that alarm goes off the FIRST thought that comes into my head is URRRGGGGGGG!

The first thought, every morning. After the best part of seven years, the old brain still fires off the "Oh no" signal. "Stay in bed, Tony. You need your rest."

After seven years. And sometimes it wins.

Most times, however my strategy wins.

I detach myself from me. And when I say me, I say the sub-standard version of me. That version we all have that doesn't want to get out bed, that doesn't want to eat well, that doesn't want to exercise, that doesn't want to grow up. The person that wants another slice of pizza. Another drink.

Can you recognise that person in you?

Each morning my strategy is simple. In many ways I detach myself from me. That old me. The one that wants to sabotage the best version of me. If I cannot detach myself, that version wins. But I give the best version of me the chance to walk away, look over his shoulder and say "come with me". Once I've moved away from the saboteur, I am able to make the best decision for me.

I get up and I go for a walk with my wife.

So don't be worried if you have the sub-standard version barking out the orders. It will continue to do so, just be aware of it. Than call it for what it is, gremlin for the best you. Then grab that vision of the best you and get up and give it everything you have got.

## Getting Grounded Gains Traction

Confidence and clarity are essential ingredients to living a life empowered. But they take a beating at times don't they? A mind full of steam, is overtaken by a head full of doubt. It happens far too often.

Strength, Confidence and Clarity is what we want but how do we get it and how do we keep it?

A tip that I have come to appreciate is our ability to get "grounded". Getting grounded helps you to gain traction in your life and your dreams. You become earthed, at one with the world, and in doing so reset the energy in your life. It's individual and it sits within us all. We just have to find whatever it is that grounds us.

Taking your shoes off and walking on the earth or the grass is one method people use. The feeling of being at one with the earth will often bring us back from the edge of anxiety, stress and doubt. Becoming grounded helps us maintain that clarity needed.

*Sometimes it's the dirt between your toes that gives you the clearest picture in your mind. Grounding yourself aligns the dirt between your toes and the vision in your mind.*

Personally, I have always felt grounded when I surf. Sitting on my board surrounded by water, provides the perfect environment for me to appreciate my life, my health, and reflect back, to freshen my perspective on life. Positive things provide strength, as does reflecting on problems and issues. Being grounded in the water provides the scope I need to refocus.

Just walking into the water has an effect that grounds me. It really is amazing and instantaneous. Whenever I needed a freshening up, I grabbed my board and head to the coast.

But it's not my only method of getting grounded.

Over the last six months, I have returned back to my home town area of the New England Tablelands in Northern New South Wales. I've been restoring some family history, and reconnecting with members of my Mum's family. We have shared good times, and good talks as we have wandered down this path of family reconnection. Which has been awesome, but my greatest take-away has been another feeling.

Driving through the area on our way to catch up with family brought a real sense of peace, of child-like wonder and recognition. I spent just eight years of my younger life in this region, but driving through towns like Tenterfield, Glen Innes, Guyra and Armidale, recognising places like Glencoe, Ben Lomond, Deepwater and Emmaville brought back all of those wonderful childhood memories. Memories of country drives with Mum and Dad, country football grounds where my Dad refereed, of delivering petrol with Dad to farmers and the people on the land. I felt completely at ease and completely at peace. I felt grounded.

Those childhood memories however, seemed larger than life. That big hill at the end of Hunter Street, Glen Innes where we used to ride our bikes, was really no more than a gentle slope. The steep slope for our billy-carts was now almost non-existent, the stream where we used to catch tadpoles was no more than a drain. The football field where I played as a junior was nowhere near as majestic as I had remembered. In fact, the town I knew was a shadow of what it was in my imagination, yet I have never felt more settled, more comfortable, more at home. The long stretches of the New England Highway of grazing land and rolling hills was another sense of grounding for me. Walking through Armidale and feeling the historic architecture was also an amazing feeling and a sense of belonging.

And the longer I stayed, the more grounded I felt. The more I dialled in, the stronger I felt. The stronger I felt, the clearer I became.

And with grounding came a real clarity of purpose. The seeds of my purpose sprouted from the Tablelands. My growth was originally fed from here. My sense of values, my sense of community; the genuine and caring approach to others were all founded here in the country side of New South Wales. This is the stuff I will never lose, but at times lose sight of. The timing was perfect.

Grounding brings strength and with strength comes a greater sense of clarity and purpose. My mind created new steps and actions. Journaling them brought them into being. A sense of calm prevailed, bringing confidence to the vision.

Grabbing traction on ideas to strengthen my business, gave me confidence to my continuing journey of empowering others. I have a purposeful journey and every day I take action to step closer to my goals and dreams. Getting grounded enabled me to grab traction.

It's fair to say, I am a driven person and have a clear purpose that I aim to live every day. Working with persistence and determination, I work towards my goals every day. But even the most driven and successful person needs time to renew and refresh, and that is why grounding is an effective tool.

Grounding helps. Grounding works. Grounding supports you. It works to eliminate the stresses and the pressures you feel at times. It works to create confidence and strength to continue your journey.

*Grounding is most effective when you have some place to go.* **When you know where you are going, grounding brings strength and confidence, when you're stagnant you get caught in the past.**

The key to being effectively grounded is to know where you are going. It is to know what you want and who it is you wish to become. It is not to wallow in the histrionics of a past life, it is not to be driven by the demons you have released, it is to provide that foundation of strength that drives you ultimately to your greatest self.

Grounding is a strategy used by many of us to achieve significant things in our lives, and it's one that can be used by you.

*Becoming grounded helps you find your purpose, your light and drive that with clarity and confidence is unbound.*

*Get grounded. Get started. Gain traction in your life*

# Getting Back Up!

Life does not ask our permission to slap us in the face. Sometimes it's hard, sometimes its gentle. Sometimes we see it coming, other times we don't.

We get slapped, we get kicked, we get knocked down. At times, it seems like an art form.

We read quotes designed to uplift us out of our doldrums and we start to feel a bit better. We put some actions in place and then life gets out the old boot again, lines us up and kicks us in the guts yet again.

We get caught in this rollercoaster as we see it. A couple of steps forward, a knockdown. More steps forward, a punch where it hurts. How can we ever get ahead we ask ourselves? If we could only get life to stop knocking us down?

How much better would life be, if you could stop the kicks in the guts? How much better would life be if you learnt to deal with the kicks?

### Dealing with the Punches

Contrary to what we may believe, it's not personal. Life doesn't have this vendetta against you. For every kick we receive, the laws of the universe suggest there should be a corresponding pat on the back. We have to learn to look for it. We have to learn to take what we can from the kick and move on. The fact that we are still standing is proof that the kick hasn't broken us.

There are two types of knock-downs that I want to talk about. The external and internal. They have similarities in how we deal with them, but the greatest impact comes from the way we view them.

How we view them is often how we deal with them. You may be in a position where every type of kick derails you and re-activate the self-sabotage behaviours we have. We take the negative route and welcome back into our lives the behaviours that keep us stuck and bound.

It is far better to take control of our emotions and how we deal with these knock-downs and it is only then can we take positive actions to better ourselves.

**External Knocks**

Sometimes we get knocked down from things outside of our control.

Examples of this may be:
- The market drops and we lose value in our superannuation
- Our company announces redundancies

- Our car gets stolen or broken into
- We get yelled at by a stranger for no reason
- We get passed over for a promotion
- The member of the opposite sex you like, likes someone else.

Some external kicks happen because of something we did. The key here is simple. Review the setback. Understand if there was anything you could have done better. Take the lesson and move on with commitment.

Most external kicks will be totally outside of your control. They happen. Understand that. What have you learnt? About people, about companies. Understand the lesson; take it and move on.

Sometimes an external kick does have some reflection for us. A missed promotion may have been due to us not being completely on our game for the considered position. Again, review, reflect and build commitment for approval for next time.

We often have no control over what happens, but we do have control over how we react and what we do moving forward. Fix what we can control, learn from what we cannot control.

## An Internal Kick in the Guts

When we cop a kick in the guts as a direct result of an action that we have done takes on a similar process. The first tip is that we cannot get into the COULDA's and SHOULDA's that we can get into. It's done, it's happened.

Again we need to review, we need to understand what we did that caused the kick, take the lesson, create a plan to improve for the future and move on. Take the lesson and improve from now. While we cannot change the kick, we can change what we do for the future.

Kicks are painful and for the pain to stop we need to stop doing what has caused the pain. When we know we caused the pain, simply, LEARN THE LESSON.

Easier said than done. Of course it is.
EVERYTHING is easier said than done. Life can be simple. But it's not easy. You need to commit to changing your life, getting better results and that happens when we take the lessons, learn from them and change our behaviours to improve future results.

If you seriously want to move to a better place, you need to become better at what we do. Allowing the kicks in the gut we get to keep us down, won't do that. We must learn to review, reflect and change our actions from our learnings. The kicks in the gut should be what we need and we need to believe that when we change our behaviours there will be an associated pat on the back coming along soon.

### Taking Control

Once you have built the platform we can now commence to move on with even greater gusto. Under the concept that life can be simple, just not easy I will now walk you through four concepts that will bring about a simple and more successful life.

Simply, it's time to take control.

### Know what you want.

***Step 1 you must know what you want.***

Sounds simple doesn't it. Know what you want. Yet for many of us, it just never happens. We know what we don't want. We don't want to be fat. We don't want a bad boss. We don't want a crappy job.

Yet we often end up overweight, with a bad boss in a crappy job. We focus on what we don't want and end up exactly with that.

Focus on what you want and your energy will feed that. Being clear about what we want and having that focus, you will surprised at what you can achieve.

Be mindful of the words we use. For example, when we use the words like; "I'm trying to achieve X" we are actually telling ourselves that we don't believe we can do it. Choose appropriate words for what you want to achieve and you will achieve.

**See yourself doing it**

***Step 2. You must be able to see it.***

Experts will tell you about the power of visualisations. And they are right. But when we are caught up in the negative, we find it hard to think anything positive about ourselves at all.

Once you know what you want, you do need to spend some time to believe that you can do it. And the best way to do that is to visualise it. Spend some time daily either as soon as you wake up or prior to going to bed, close your eyes and visualise yourself doing what you want to do.

The science behind this can be explained simply. Our brains are naturally resistant to change. I believe this is a protective measure but it keeps us bound in the place of

our comfort. By using visualisation techniques and"
seeing" what you can do, the brain becomes less resistant
to that event.

Take the next step and start the process of
visualising what you want. Once you believe you can do
it, you are then ready for the next stage

.

**Map out your actions**

*Step 3. Start taking action to where you want to be.*

What stops most people in their tracks. It's not the
dreaming, we all have dreams. It's not the visioning
process. It's usually the hard part of the equation. The part
where we need to create action.

Before we create action we need to map it out and get
it written down. Like a road map, we need to create a path
for our journey. What are the steps we need to take to get
closer to where we want to be? What is our first step?
What is our next step? What do we need to start doing? Is
there anything we need to stop doing?

Every day we need to aim to be closer to where we
want to be. At this moment you are the farthest you will
ever be from where you want to be. That's ONLY if you
start taking action. Every day you take action, you will get
closer to where you want to be.

**Keep it in front of you**

*Step 4- Keep it clearly in front of you.*

We now know what we want. We can see ourselves doing it and we have mapped out our actions and started moving towards our dreams.

Our greatest challenge now is to keep the goal visual. Keep it in front of us. How we do that is our own choice.

Some will pin it to a corkboard, put it on their fridge, post-it note on the bathroom mirror or set reminders and actions on their smart phone.

The key is to keep it in front of you. Keep it in the forefront of everything you do.

**Know yourself**

*Step 5. Know Yourself and keep yourself on track with conscious gauges*

The final step is to know you. Ask yourself the following?

- What has stopped you in the past?

- Why is achieving what you want important to you?
- What is likely to stop you?

When you have a better understanding of yourself you can set some conscious thought gauges to help you get to where you want to be. We are blessed with conscious thought and this is our greatest tool we have to keep us motivated as we face the inevitable hurdles that will come our way.

As you build momentum, keep asking yourself every time you do something "Is this hurting me or is this helping me?"

**Summary**

Life doesn't ask for permission to slap you in the face. It just slaps you in the face, and when it does, the steps outlined below will allow you to deal with that kick in the guts appropriately.

1. Know what you want
2. See yourself doing it
3. Map out actions and get started
4. Keep the goal in front of you
5. Know yourself and use gauges to keep you on track

Life will kick you in the guts. It's our choice to stay down. One rule that I have always had, is that when a bad thing happens allow yourself some "down time". But never allow that to go for longer than 24 hours. Then get back moving forward. I also believe the same when we win. Celebrate, no longer than 24 hours and get moving again.

Follow these steps and you will always keep moving forward even though life keeps kicking you in the guts. Get moving. You deserve it.

## STRONGER BRAVER WISER

## Simply Musing – I Wonder

I often wonder what would happen if we all just stopped. We consciously stop all the hustle, all the grind, all the quest for bullshit business grandiose, all the shit of the laptop beachside business ideal that the majority must find so appealing. We chose to stop the relentless pursuit of power and manipulation, the marketing machines that keep us wanting more.

And I wonder what would happen if we just started appreciating who you are, who you're with, who you deal with and what you want authentically, away from the hype. What if we became happy with what we had? What would that world look like?

I wonder what would happen? Would the world as we know it just grind to a halt or would it just create a new beginning

*"When will you open your eyes to the possibility of the world?"*


*"Where you are and what you have been through has you perfectly placed to move forward. Stronger, Braver, Wiser."*


*"Who lives inside your head? The hero of your story OR the victim of someone else's?"*


*"The pain of the journey should challenge you to make change, the vision of what could be drives you forward."*


*"I'm grateful for today. I am stronger, braver, wiser."*

*"Your self-imposed prison. That thing called your COMFORT ZONE. Challenge it, stretch it. You will thank yourself."*

*"How many good ideas have you let go because you didn't believe in yourself? You have to believe to achieve!"*

*"If you're too busy being angry at the world, don't be surprised when the world returns serve."*

*"Don't imprison yourself through self-doubt. Break out of your self-imposed prison with intentional action."*

*"Isn't it time you chose to be remarkable?"*

"Stop aiming at being average. The world deserves your best. Stop flying under the radar, playing safe. Aim to be your best."

"If you're tired of being unhappy and unhappy with being tired. Realise the choices that you make reflect the way you feel. How would life be better if you could feel sensational. Make the choice, make the change."

"If you believe that life is a game. Get good at it. Set up well and go your hardest."

"Keep punching. Keep getting up. You won't be beaten."

*"We search for happiness in things and people. The old "I will be happy when" syndrome. Look at the things to be grateful for and happiness follows."*

*"A decision… A Choice…. That's where it starts."*

*"Are you cocooned by comfort or ready to break free to be the best you?"*

*"Stop putting your effort into excuses. Put it into results."*

*"Enjoy the journey, but stay focussed on the dream."*

## Congratulations: You have Resistance

"How can I be the best me? I have so many things against me, Tony. You don't understand what I've been through/going-through / my family / my partner / my work / my responsibility / my stress / the pressure/ my life."

Congratulations, you have resistance.

What?

Congratulations, you have resistance.

Why is that congratulations?

It means you are moving. The only things that don't have resistance are dead. The sheer fact that you are moving requires resistance. To move one way will always have contrasting forces. To move towards greatness, the forces against you will seem insurmountable. But, standing here today, is testament to your 100% success rate in surviving the resistance you have encountered previously.

The law of resistance. CoachCurl style. Let us not be confused with the Law of Resistance, with all of its formulas and detail, that provides the basis of electric generation. Let us also acknowledge the Law of

Resistance that fits within the Law of Attraction mode, the one that says we resist at times the very things that we wish to attract because it is not our primary focus. Two very valid and valuable Laws.

The CoachCurl Law of Resistance is a validation tool. It validates our journey and reinforces our direction. But to fully allow the law to work, we must continue on our path. If we choose to turn back from the resistance, it then conspires to hold us in a resentful and unhappy pattern of existence, not living.

Allow me to illustrate. A number of years back, I undertook a change in wellness and healthy living and as a result lost 20 kilograms over a six-month period. I took charge of the way I lived, what I ate and regulated coping strategies that allowed me to bring about physical change. After a while that change became noticeable amongst friends and colleague and the compliments flew. For a short time, then the resistance came. Instead of compliments I started hearing comments like:

- How much more weight do you want to lose?
- Surely you are still not on a diet?
- You look good the way you are now, don't lose any more weight. You will be too skinny.
- I've seen AIDS patients look better than you. (my personal favourite)

The resistance says more about the other person than it ever said about me. Through my discipline and desire, I challenged people to their very core, they felt inferior based on my results and as a consequence they desired the status quo to return to make them feel better. Many will listen to the resistance, and reduce their efforts.

If I had listened to the resistance, that exact same thing would have happened. A return to the status quo, a return to an unhealthy life and an unhappy me.

Instead that resistance validated my results and the results, and the motivation for them. They kept me moving forward, pushing against the barriers to burst through the other side. The other side is a beautiful thing and what awaited me was the Law of Momentum. When you hit the Law of Momentum, a beautiful thing happens. Habits form, motivation increases, results continue. Change becomes easier.

Resistance is good, whenever you attempt change for the better in your life, to move onwards from your current situation, you will face resistance. And congratulations for that.

And that resistance is a sneaky thing. The obvious stuff is the external. The less obvious is the stuff that goes through your own head. The self-talk that challenges you, tries to persuade you to stand down, to take the path well-travelled and comfortable with.

Don't try and reason with your internal resistance. Instead, vision it out of existence by visualising the life you want and then feeding that emotion with action. Create energy around your vision and that energy will over-ride the negative energy that potentially occurs with your own doubtful self-talk. Channel your energy to where it's best used, to overcome the internal resistance we feel and build your better job.

Falling victim to an internal hatchet job doesn't serve anyone well.

The only thing you build sitting on the couch is your "bum groove". The only thing you build when comfortable in a life that you have accepted, is resistance to your dreams and goals and acceptance for what you have settled for.

So again, congratulations. If you are feeling resistance to positive change, that's awesome. It's validating you are on the right path. Everything worthwhile is only achieved after pushing through resistance.

Validate your direction, verify your results. Make resistance work for you by motivating you to continue the path you are on, to continue the journey to your very best. To continue on to where you previously feared to go.

The equation I would like to share is the one that follows. Reflect back every time you feel resistance attempting to persuade you from your path.

Life can be simple, it ain't easy. So don't take the easy option. Challenge the resistance, challenge yourself, become great.

Positive response to Resistance.

- Resistance felt = validation of results + renewed motivation + continued forward motion = momentum and continued results.

Negative response to Resistance

- Resistance felt = acceptance of resistance + wilting of desire + reduced effort to forward motion = loss of momentum and return to status quo or worse.

Congratulations, you have resistance. Simply, don't let it win.

## Simply Musing – The Pathway of Choice

We are all on a pathway. For some it's a pathway to success, for others it leads to destruction. For many it's a journey of the mundane where the quest for safety and security from the threats and fears of others perceptions and opinions. Which pathway are you on? The pathway we choose is a choice we make. But it's more than a choice. We must choose to act on that choice.

I shared this on my Facebook Page after sitting in an airport people-watching waiting for my flight.

Where is your choice taking you?

"I am better today because I've learnt from my mistakes. I'm stronger today because of the pain I have endured. I can love today because of the times my heart has been broken. I can trust today because of the times that trust has been shattered. I can grow today because of the years I stood still. I have purpose today because of my years spent wandering. I have faith in me today because of the years that fear overrode me. I matter. You matter. Your life matters. What has happened you cannot change. Where you are is where you are: best place to step towards the very best version of you. You are not what happens to you, you choose to be who you are."

"If I always stuck up for what I had, I would have missed the most amazing *things I have today. What are you fighting for that you need to let go? Release the magic within. The magic of what could be."*

*"Belief helps create action, action can change your world."*

*"Nothing great happens in the comfort zone, so know your strengths and play there."*

*"Punch out your potential and your promise every day."*

*"Today and every day. What will you do today to get closer to your dreams and*

goals? What must you do every day to build your success."

"Only when you decide to take decisive action does your life improve. You are better than what you have settled for, what you have been conditioned to believe. Reach for the stars, reach for the goals and get going."

It's tough staying the course, but the tough stay the course."

"One thing I can assure you, life is not easy, but it can be simple. Focus on what's important and don't let your distractions derail you."

"Take a seat and take it all in as another day of potential and promise awakes. The GLORIOUSNESS of it all. Glad to be alive and embracing everything that it encompasses. Embrace life, embrace your dreams, take action, fulfilling your destiny. You are here for a reason. Live your purpose, love your very essence of being."

"The day begins with promise and ends beautifully when you realise that same promise"

# Addicted to Distraction

### Celebrate Stillness and Silence

Distractions derail. We live in a world of constant distraction. As a race, we find it increasingly hard to shut off. Research tells us our smart phone is often the last thing we use prior to going to sleep, and often the first thing we touch on waking.

And, in our moments of quiet, we are more likely to reach for that same smartphone.

Whereas once we used those times to reach inside us and embrace stillness. Allowing ourselves to be alone with our thoughts, and senses, our stillness. It's different now.

We have become addicted to distraction.

We can't even walk down the street without being glued to our smartphone screen. Even a visit to the toilet usually is not the solitary destination it used to be. The number of people who take calls on the toilet is horrifying, a fact rammed home from some recent travels. Heaven forbid. Nothing appears to be sacred anymore.

Boredom sets in quicker and quicker. Our need to be entertained, working or simply distracted appears to be unquenched. Entertained by mindless activity, mindless scrolling of our social media feeds.

What an incredible shame, the days of accepting stillness appear to be almost over. Our minds are constantly firing, bringing sleepless nights, overtired days and constant connection. Scrolling through our social media feed, a mindless activity, we now do while watching TV, having dinner, being with friends. That constant buzz of a notification, the ding of a message feeds the addiction and we are seldom unconnected.

The beauty of stillness and silence is it allows us to reach within ourselves, without distraction. It helps centre us, it helps bring the inner person to the centre and helps us become whole. It allows us to be alone, and embrace true reflection.

Whether that is in silent spiritual prayer, in mindful meditation or simple staring out to sea or over the countryside, the ability to celebrate stillness and silence helps us become the person we are designed to be.

It helps us see the beauty and clarity of our own thoughts, and for that moment we become timeless. The beauty within us comes into focus and we allow ourselves to be our inner champion. How good is that.

Staying conscious of the beauty that surrounds us is another opportunity. Each moment we view happens just in that moment. The waves crashing, the water flowing, the birds flying, the wind rustling the leaves, each moment is significant by itself and won't happen again. Each moment is viewed for the first and only time, how can we ever get jaded by that.

But we do. In a world of extremism, marketing and fluffy cat videos, the solitude and beauty of stillness appears to be a spent currency. Each moment exists in itself. We have just forgotten how to embrace it.

Celebrating silence and stillness allows us to feel the significance of ourselves and the world around. Being alone with yourself and to see things clearly for the first time, is a true gift that you can give yourself. Those that have a system of stillness, are centred to face the world that evolves faster with every day. People who can celebrate stillness and silence are never alone. Additionally, they are never lonely, as they have that capacity to be at one with themselves.

Our distracted digital world is here to stay, so the question is more of how we can truly embrace the beauty that is the stillness and the silence.

Think about dis-connecting from our digital world. Digitally, turn off, turn on silence and vibration and take some time for yourself. Embrace the morning, watch the sun come up as often as you can, and enjoy the colours of the sun set. Take the time to see something for the first time or to challenge yourself to see something new from something routine.

Give thanks every morning and share quiet reflection every night. The important thing, take time to turn off and look inward.

Take the time to celebrate stillness and silence and see the joy that the world can bring, simply.

## Simply Musing - The Beauty of You

If the marketing world around us ceases to exist today. If the media world did the same. If all the social media networks stopped, the world of emotions and feelings for many would simply stop. There would be nothing out there to check in to, feel bad about, get angry about or expand energy on. Except you would still exist, the waves would still crash on the shoreline, the trees would still grow towards the sun, the sun would still rise and the sun would still set. The people close to you would still be there and YOU would still exist. What does that existence look like? Free from controlling and competing environments that keep us bound, angry, depressed, sad and unhappy. Could you free yourself from the chains of the oppressors and learn to live in the beauty of YOU?

*"Our thoughts affect our agreement with reality, our story we tell ourselves. IF you want to change your story, start with your thoughts."*

*"You don't have to compete against the best to be your best. Just compete against your best."*

*"The lure of your long term satisfaction, must be greater than the lure of your short term gratification."*

*"It's happened. It's in the past. You can't change it. You are not broken. Learn from the past, then build from it."*

*"Not asking questions: Giving up on your dreams: Settling for less than you deserve causes you pain, a pain owned by the majority. Be among the few who are inquisitive, forge plans to chase their dreams and take intentional action to live the life aligned with their potential."*

*"Your story should inspire others. Your journey should inspire you."*

*"Have people in your life who feed your dream, and nurture reality."*

*"Toxic people sell you short. When you listen to them, you give them power, that's when you sell yourself short."*

*"Growing up I always had second hand surfboards and boardshorts, but Mum always made sure my school uniforms were new. It was her way of showing me what's important."*

*"True friends see the life in your eyes and hear the smile in your voice."*

*"We all have a story within us, mine just includes dancing to "Rebel Yell" at the Court Jester."*

*"Your mind is powerful and so are your thoughts. Ultimately they determine the life you lead, the success you have, what you settle for. It manifests your agreement with reality. Just like the wolves, what you feed wins."*

*"Our agreement with reality dictates what we see in the world. Our agreement is why some see the magic, some see the deception while others see the con. Many things influence your agreement with reality, but only you can change it."*

## Well, It Won't Happen Here.
## Forever Etched in My Mind.


I didn't see it coming.

Sometimes life throws a punch which we don't see coming. Punches that come without even a hint. This was one of those times. Working for a large retail store in North Queensland as a Department Manager, I usually only spoke with our District Manager, Ray, when he toured my department, but today was different. He had requested a meeting. What? That never happens and it was a bit concerning for me.

What could he want? What have I done? Was I in trouble? What's going on? I had seen redundancies in recent times within the company, and those made redundant hadn't seen it coming. This was not good.

Talk about negative thoughts!

I knew this wasn't normal. After all, I had been doing this role in the store for five and a half years. I knew normality. I knew routine. I knew this was not normal. And it worried the heck out of me.

I was numb as I walked towards the office. Uncertain, nervous and in all honesty a bit confused. The door was open and Ray was inside with my Store Manager, Maurie. Ray was seated to the side of the manager's desk so I sat down next to him. Thankfully, Ray got straight to the point.

"Tony, have you ever thought about being a Store Manager?"

From initial deflation to instant inflation. From seemingly holding my breath inside, not daring to breathe, to an outpouring of relief. The pressure valve released and cocky, young Tony returned I breathed again.

"Of course, Ray, I would love to be a Store Manager" I replied, as if this was the most natural conversation I should be having. My confidence had returned and I felt great. Wow, they want to make me a Store Manager. Awesome.

"Well it won't happen here." Ray continued. The air sucked out of me again, as I waited on his next words.

"It won't happen in North Queensland., Tony. We need to get you back to Brisbane" "Ok", I stammered. "I would need to talk with Sharon"

And with that, my life that I had come to know and love, was turned upside down.

Rewind back five and half years. I had arrived in Townsville, as a young up and coming manager, hell-bent of enjoying my "country stint" It was accepted that managers had to do a "country stint" before they could move on and become a Store Manager. I was 22, I was ambitious and I wanted to enjoy the stint. It was 1988.

Fast forward back to the present time, and I was very comfortable being a North Queensland boy. I met Sharon, the girl of my dreams, stole her away from another Tony when I got the chance, we bought our first house, got married and had our son, Tim. The ambitious young man, had certainly matured, was accepted into Sharon's large family and basically was enjoying his time as a married man and young father. The two years had stretched into five and a half years without any drama at all. It just happened, and I was pretty comfortable and happy with that.

Now, it was all being turned around, upside down, inside out and in every way imaginable. This was tough.

The discussion that night was intense, only surpassed by the events of the month that followed. Sharon was amazingly supportive, considering she was the one giving up everything. Losing the physical support of her family was huge. Sharon's family was large, being one of 11 siblings and one thing we had come to cherish was the instant party a family gathering could become, with young and old kids alike enjoying our time together. Having her Mum close by was always handy for us with Tim.

Leaving the emotion of our first home was also so evident. It was our first home we bought together. The home we came home to after being married. The home we brought Tim home to after his birth. It was our home. The emotions and the feelings were real and she was leaving them to provide me with hope for my career. I was blessed to have her amazing support.

But we had to face reality. Preparing our house for sale was high on the agenda, to finish all of the renovations we wanted to do, with the bitter-sweet reality of having the home we wanted, only to sell it and hand it to someone else to enjoy.

Researching real estate in Brisbane was equally interesting and frustrating, with Sharon having little idea of the city and the best places to live. Decisions had to be made on where we lived, and as Sharon and I were moving to stores on opposite sides of the city, we chose to live closer to Sharon's work and into a new area for me.

We moved through our "must-do's" with optimism and energy. While doing so, we spent many late nights simply talking and planning our new life coming up. These nights brought us closer, a strong foundation we needed for the year we would face.

These conversations really built the strength for our life together from that day forward, through great times and tough.

It was frightening. It was exciting. It was incredibly real.

In the end, timing was perfect. Our house sold with the contract finalised, just days before we were due to fly out. We had just under a week of catching our breath at Sharon's Parents place, before a final tearful farewell to a life we loved so much. A final wave and wiping away a tear as Sharon carried Tim up the airplane stairs. We took our seats, tightly held each other's hands and smiled grimly. Sharon looked out the window until she lost sight of the city of her birth, the city of her family, which was the city of Townsville. Symbolically when she lost sight, she faced forward in her seat and went over the plans for the remainder of the day.

That day with Ray, changed our lives dramatically. We had to rebuild a friend network, we had to rebuild our support foundation, we had to become independent and strong within. Our first year in Brisbane was our toughest EVER as we faced our tears, we faced our fears as well as facing the celebration of our daughter Tayla joining us and me getting the promotion I had worked for. That year we found us.

That year created our fight and resilience. It made us stronger, braver and wiser, setting us up for success together as a family. And since then, every new step we have taken we have done as a team, knowing that together we can face anything. We know that new levels do not come from standing still, they don't come from being comfortable. We know that if we want better, we have to be better, we have to do better.

Often I hear Ray say as I dream about something new and amazing. "Well it won't happen here". And that compels me to get my backside into gear and get going, with intensity, energy and anticipation.

What are you dreaming of and maybe scaring you a little bit? Get moving because:

"It won't happen here"

## Simply Musing – Playing Well with Others

Some say I don't play with others; maybe I just haven't found the right "others". I have recently stopped playing with others for a number of different reasons. The main kicker is the feeling of shared values, a common sense of purpose and underlying lack of trust. At the same time, working with others who give and share freely, and of who the contributions are appreciated and loved. Being a team, compared to not being a team. Individuals forced to work together.

At times, don't be forced to play nice with others, especially when their version of playing nice favours them, and is focused on them. Playing nice means working together for a shared result. I'm not sorry for not being able to play nice with everyone, sometimes I only play nice with the best.

*"There is no doubt that sometimes we hit the ground, and we hit the ground hard. When we get hit the hardest, is when we bounce back the strongest."*

*"Most of the time the road is not clear ahead. We have roadblocks and obstacles and stumble because of them. Are you courageous enough to map your way around them and continue on?"*

*"We have everything within us for our greatness and for our destruction. It comes back to what we think about."*

*"Having a team deliver standards and performance is much easier when they want to be there and want to be led by you."*

*"Who brings out the champion in you?
Those that help you be the hero of your
story, keep them close."*

*"Calling it as you see it, should include*

*yourself as well."*

*"Empower your possibility with the power
of*

*your promise."*

*"The importance of "small wins.*

*"When we believe that we can win it's
amazing how positive we can become."*

*"So, to make positive change, plan small
wins along the way."*

*"It's hard getting momentum riding a bike up hill... It's hard getting momentum when you're dragging around all the pain from your past."*

*"Today is your day. The day you take control to become the best version of you."*

*"Smiles are such a simple thing to give but means so much to many."*

*"Choosing the right people to surround you, and letting go of the wrong ones, takes courage. Be courageous!"*

*"Your ego can be a wonderful ally or your worst enemy. If your ego drives you to exceed standards, beat yesterday, and be better than what you would otherwise do*

*... That's awesome but stay humble. If your ego is more concerned with how you look to others, then stops you achieving for fear of looking*
*stupid or even worse, failing...*
*Well that is just dumb. Drive standards, be aware of who you are, understand what drives you, be aware of your core values, your purpose your vision."*

*"Set your intention focus on purpose. Drive it forward with action."*

## Tomorrow Never Comes Until You Make Tomorrow Today

I remember the day well. I know where I was, I knew who I was with. A day that should have been celebration, became a day of devastation.

We were at our neighbour's house, having a backyard barbecue. I was there with my two brothers, Geoffrey and David, as we waited news on our new baby brother. Dad had taken mum to hospital and even though things didn't look good, I remember being hopeful.

Just after dark, dad returned home. He gathered us three boys together and shared the news that we were not wanting to hear. Our little brother didn't make it. Jason Ian, had been born as a "blue blood" baby and in those times, all care was taken but little chance of survival. December 17, 1972. Birth and death date for Jason Ian Curl.

He was placed into an unmarked grave. I cannot remember if there was a ceremony or not. I am not sure what support my mother received at the time, if any. I don't recall tears, fights or anything after the death. I just remember an overwhelming sense of normality return.

I was young, yes, and we lived then in different times. If there was sorrow and sadness evident it was done privately. I do know my two brothers and I were devastated on that first night and our tears flowed easily, but that's it in terms of pain. Normality returned, very quickly.

And Jason lay in an unmarked grave.

We moved away just over a year later to the beachside town of Maroochydore. And my third brother, Malcolm, was born three years later. As a family we settled in to beach living and started forging independent lives of our own. Our lives took many turns and corners over the years, and Mum and Dad would often speak of placing a stone for Jason and marking his grave. But as life moved on, it never became a priority.

Still, Jason lay in an unmarked grave.

We moved to Brisbane in 1979, and I started High School. Geoffrey joined the Air Force and David and I got caught up in our sports. Dad passed away in 1987. Geoff got married, divorced, remarried and divorced, David got married as did I in 1991. Life took over and while we always had the intention of marking Jason's resting spot, it always seemed to be a thing for tomorrow.

Still, Jason lay in an unmarked grave.

Mum died after her battle with cancer, in November 2011. As part of her final wishes she wanted Jason to be laid with her. Symbolically we brought soil back from Jason unmarked grave, and now Jason rests with mum and dad. Geoffrey and I made a vow to mark Jason's grave. After almost 40 years, Jason deserved better.

Still Jason lay in an unmarked grave.

We had all had good intentions. We all wanted to do the right thing, but we just couldn't make our way to get it done. It was always earmarked for tomorrow. And tomorrow simply never came. Until such time someone made tomorrow, today, Jason was destined, like many, to lie forever in an unmarked grave.

Have you ever walked around a cemetery and noticed the number of unmarked graves? Forgotten members of families, forgotten sons and daughters, forgotten lovers, wives and husbands. Unmarked, lost in history.

In August, 2015, Jason Ian finally got recognition. Sharon and I, made tomorrow today and planned a weekend away in Glen Innes. We bundled all the good intentions from my family and finally delivered a memorial for Jason Ian. With us came, a nice piece of rock, some bags of pebbles and a stainless steel plaque.

After 42 years, Jason was finally memorialised. He can finally rest in peace.

I share this story simply as a reminder that until plans are made and actions done, tomorrow never comes. Our family always had the best intentions to commemorate Jason Ian, we just never got around to doing it. If it's important it should get done. We just need to see the importance.

Sharon and I have already been back once, since that initial trip. Our plan is now to return every six months and add to the memorial every time. Our challenge remains to plan and do it. We know it's important, but sometimes important stuff gets missed when life gets in the way. So we need to be disciplined to ensure we carry through with our actions.

Just as we all should with everything that is important in our lives. Every family has a skeleton or two, every relationship has important things left unsaid. Every career has important tasks and effort being held back. For when? Tomorrow.

What are you waiting for tomorrow to do? To get done? To achieve? To start? Where your good intentions are disconnecting from the actions you should do for the things you desire?

Can you see tomorrow? can you touch tomorrow? Can you feel tomorrow? No, only when you make tomorrow today. The only time is when you make tomorrow today. Make it count. Make it memorable.

Don't dwell on the reasons it has taken your so long. Don't live in the realm of regrets and remorse. Be thankful for the fact that you have started by making tomorrow today and that first step will always represent the biggest step. Your first step leads to the next, which leads to the next and continues doing so until something is achieved. Don't be derailed by the negative emotions. Straighten that resolve and your jawline and get moving.

What within you lies in that symbolic unmarked grave? How can you create the memorial to you and your best life and effort? Make tomorrow today and make today count.

## Life Isn't Fair – Get Over It.

Tears and the words "Life isn't fair" are a common occurrence in the world.

What I want to know is who said it is supposed to be?

Daily we see millions born around the world. Some will have what may be viewed as disabilities......but I've come to believe that we all have our own disabilities to overcome.

It's not fair that people are born with more talent than discipline and dedication.

It's not fair that people are born with more discipline and dedication than talent.

It's not fair that some are born into privileged positions in life?

It's not fair that some of our greatest minds are potentially born into some of our lowest demographics.

Get the point?

Life isn't fair! Full stop. Get over the concept that it is.

I find once we acknowledge this, life gets simpler.

We all have gifts; we all have a purpose, that's why we are here. My purpose isn't your purpose. And your purpose isn't mine.

If we live in the way of longing for what we don't have, we miss the potential of what we do have.

I heard Nick Vujicic speak in Orlando, February 2014. Nick is an inspiration, and shares his journey of hope around the world. Nick was born without arms and legs. Certainly a case of life isn't fair. Nick highlights his emotions in his best-selling books and speaking engagements, and how he deals with them. He found his calling and purpose and now gives people hope and inspiration daily as he spreads his message.

Life isn't fair.

I was born with some talent at sport, but I was also born without the discipline needed to maximise that potential. **Life's not fair**. I saw lesser talented people, with greater discipline achieve better results and achieve greater success. Regret was a common theme for me, and only when I could acknowledge my shortcomings did I stop the pain of regret.

The world is full of talented alcoholics. Many barstools are taken up with people living the life of "I coulda been a contender". Life's not fair.

When we realise that, is when we acknowledge to do the best we have <u>with what we have</u>. If I was to compare my life against the success of players that I competed with and against in my youth, I would be in a constant spiral of regret and blame.

But I acknowledge that I needed to learn discipline and dedication. And when I did it was too late to utilise my sporting talent. No-one signs sporting stars as rookies in their forties.

- Life's not fair that others pigeonhole you on your past mistakes
- Life's not fair that people don't see you for the potential you have, but for the perception they have.
- Life's not fair that some seem to get a favoured run through life
- Life's not fair that people who seem to lack basic human care obtain positions of power over us
- Life's not fair that at times our results are dictated by others
- Life's not fair......... we could fill a book (and maybe I will)

When you acknowledge that life's not fair, it helps simplify your life and builds a base to build the best version of yourself. Accept that not everyone gets the same breaks. Accept that some have natural talent greater than you in certain areas.

You start maximising what you have, instead of worrying what you don't have.

But do not accept the fact that this provides an out! Do not accept the fact that this is an excuse for not achieving your potential. NO WAY.

Acknowledge that life's not fair and dig in and work every day at what you want to achieve.

Maximise your potential. Build on what you have! You cannot build on what you don't have.

## Stop Cheating on Life

A lot of people are wearing "activity trackers" to help them gain health and fitness and I am now one of them. They provide a visual measurement on how physically active we have been for the day and an additional spur to become more active to burn our caloric intake. They are a great tool to help you achieve your goals.

They are also happened to be a great conversation starter. I have found others wearing these trackers have opened up conversations with me over the last four weeks in many places. Many of these stories have been uplifting, while others highlight the inadequacies that we have as human beings. I had a number of women tell me how their husbands have found a way to register "steps" by just moving or waving their arms. (why is it always the husbands?)

**They found a way to cheat.**

But they may be showing they are active BUT they are not accomplishing anything!

Which leads me to this line of thought.

*"Activity alone is not accomplishment"*

So why do people cheat? Why do they have to find a way to defeat the program?

To me it's because of three simple facts.

1. We are in a competition with someone.
2. We don't want to look bad.
3. We don't own the goal.

From my experience, I understand that goals will only work when we do. When we own the goal we will do better than if we simply "accept" the goal. When we accept the goal, we often create a lot of "activity" but little accomplishment. We want to be "seen" doing the right thing, not necessarily doing the right thing. You need to be taking the RIGHT STEPS towards your goal, not just any step.

So here are my five ways to ensure you are taking the RIGHT STEPS towards your goals.

1. **Know what you want**.

Sounds simple, right. Yet, we often don't know what we want. **Instead we often say what we don't want, and that's what we focus on.** But we need to know what we want and then we focus on it. The magic happens when we focus on that. Our attention is real, our actions become determined and we start making it happen. Be specific, be clear, know exactly what you want with the goal.

## 2. Make a plan

The first part of action must be to write the goal down and the put your plan together. What is your first step? What is the next step? What are the daily steps that need to change to ensure you reach your goal? What is your goal? Get it all on paper and get your goal-plan, your map together.

## 3. Know your path

Understand what it will take to get to where you wish to go. We all know we can drive from Brisbane to Perth, but we cannot do it in a day, no matter how good we are. Attempting to do so will end in failure.

With everything worth achieving you need to understand the path you have to take. Add this to your map. Know the path well.

## 4. Celebrate the Small Steps

Along the way take time to acknowledge your progress. At the end of each day review your steps and ask yourself. "Did today help me or hurt me?" If you took the right steps, pat yourself on the back and celebrate a little. If it hurt you, correct it for tomorrow.

## 5. Map your way around the roadblocks.

Along the path, you will surely come across

roadblocks and obstacles. Maybe the same ones that have stopped you in the past. But today is different. Map your way around that roadblock. Look for another point on your map that you can work towards to work your way around the block. Like that road-trip to Perth, if one road is blocked, you would look for another way. There are always other ways to get to a set place. Just because your preferred path is blocked, doesn't mean your goal is.

**Take the right steps.**

Activity is not accomplishment. I am sure you know people who are always busy but rarely accomplishing or successful in what they do. And while we will often be focused and determined to achieve, we can also be our own worst enemies as we listen to our own excuses and stop. You would be hard pressed to find one person in history who was singularly driven and solely responsible for their own success. You need to look for those that will motivate, inspire, challenge and support you. If you don't have them, look for them. Because:

### *"Environment is stronger than will"*

Ask yourself.

1. Who is around me that supports yet challenges me to succeed?
2. Analyse why you didn't achieve in the past and ask yourself "What's Changed?

3. Am I taking the RIGHT STEPS or am I just being active for the sake of being active?

Stop cheating on life. Stop laying low, stop flying under the radar. You are designed to be the very best you can be. It's only when we embrace this, and make changes to our life can we ever truly succeed on our terms.

**STRONGER BRAVER WISER**

## Our Legacy from a Special Boy Carter

26th May, 2013 a brave little boy lost his fight and left a close knit family network reeling and looking for answers. Grasping for answers.

Carter Desmond was that little boy. Born just four weeks earlier, his fight for life started at the beginning. He fought infection. He fought sickness. He fought internal organs that wouldn't work. He fought a heart that wouldn't function. He faced almost daily operations. He fought bravely for every day of his short life. Until that day, when he lost the fight.

Life can be unfair and answers were nowhere to be found.

Carter left a legacy. The impact he left was immense. The extended family and friend's community rallied around the young couple, who were simply a rock throughout. Understandably the grief was obvious, but from the grief came a legacy.

A new resolve was born when Carter passed. Carter had only known love in his short time with us. And from that love came the legacy. The legacy of Carter.

You find your own meaning when there are no answers. Life isn't fair. Four week olds' aren't meant to leave us. They are not meant to pass away. Four weeks of fight, fighting for the very basic tenements of life, that so many of us take for granted. He fought to breathe by himself. He fought for his organs to work by themselves. He fought for his heart to beat.

Yet how many of us have given up on life, and have all those things that Carter fought for.

Are you fighting for your life?

Are you creating a legacy?

Carter did. This year will see a fund-raising lunch in memory of Carter, earn much needed funds for a children's hospital charity. We know that this lunch will become an annual event and will grow.

But this is only part of the legacy. Those impacted from Carter are living the legacy daily. Carter forced those close to face up to the lives they were living. They have stopped settling for second best. They have stopped taking life for granted. They have become more grateful for every gift of a day they are given. They understand that life is frail and can be taken in an instant.

They now:
- Live life to the fullest. Maximise their potential. Don't take the basics of life for granted
- Love friends and family unconditionally
- Chase their dreams

You may not have known Carter, but you can take on his legacy.

**Live Life. Fight for life. Every day is a gift.
Don't take it for granted.**

## 99.7%

So much research indicates that we are controlled by our subconscious actions and thoughts. Some have estimated that this is as high as 99.7% of our daily functioning is driven by our subconscious. That's an amazing stat. 99.7% of what we do daily is controlled subconsciously. That includes our breathing, our heartbeats and blood circulation, but it also includes our habits that have formed and control much of our thoughts and views on the world.

Our habits make or break us. Most of us acknowledge that, however I am not sure that we actually realise the seriousness in relation to our habits. We are truly on Auto-Pilot in so many ways when it comes to us living. The quality of our Auto-Pilot determines the quality of our life.

This auto-pilot also helps determines our agreement with reality. It defines the way we think and feel, it defines our success and failures, it defines our view on life. It defines the story we tell ourselves. Our agreement with reality has links to our perception, it aligns with our perspective. It defines us.

There is good news. We still have conscious thought. And our agreement of reality can be changed by ourselves. Our view of the world can be changed by what we <u>tell ourselves</u>. You don't have to be stuck with it. If you are unhappy with your view of the world, it can be changed but does requires action, effort and persistence.

So stop telling yourself crap. Stop putting garbage in, garbage out.

Stop telling yourself, Same crap, different day

Here are some tips to make the 99.7% work for you.

Start focusing on what is good in your life. No matter how small...by focusing on the positive you start to change your view to positive. And by thinking positive, you start to attract the positive.

Affirm yourself daily. Make a daily agenda item with yourself. Analyse the good things that happen every day. Recognise the positives and make plans for more tomorrow. Look for the good in every situation.

Take action to break bad habits. Get out and go for a walk. Be fully present with loved ones. If people come to whinge, politely refuse to be part of their plan to offload pain into your life.

The fact is, we can all do this. And many other strategies are out there. Do you want to share yours?

# Are you Clocking off from Life?

Have you clocked off? Have you retired from life?
Have you stopped having a go?

Have you chosen to accept what life has given you,
or are you choosing to create your life? There is a
powerful difference.

When you choose to create your life: you learn and
grow, live with fulfilment and your life becomes a
joyful journey. When you choose to accept your
life, you become focused on enduring your life,
watching the clock and making it through every
dreary day.

*"Life is not meant to be an endurance event, its
meant to be an exciting journey of enhancement."*

Many people have stopped growing. When you stop
growing, you stop living. Many have stopped living
and now just bide their time before it becomes
official.

Sometimes, our lives, are turned around in
upheaval, through catastrophic events both natural,
and caused by others. Outside of our control,
outside of our actions. Negative impacts caused by
other things. When faced with this, we still have
choices to make.

Is it really that simple? The choices we make?

How many times have we heard someone comment " That person has a great attitude" when interviewed after a natural disaster as they piece together the remnants of what was once their life? They are choosing not to focus on the negative but to be constructive in their thoughts. They are not dwelling on what they lost, but on how to regather, how to reconstruct, how to survive and how to thrive. To do otherwise is counterproductive.

They make the best choices they can. So yes, I do believe it can be simple. Sometimes, we have no choice in what happens to us...we choose how we react and respond.

Where are you? Are you making the choices to make your life fulfilling? Are you making the choices that enable intentional learning? Do you challenge yourself every day? Do you know how?

One last point! Do you bet on yourself? If not, why not? If you can't bet on yourself, don't blame others when they don't. Care and support others, but care and support yourself first.

Don't clock off from life, you are still standing and that is testament there is more to live. Embrace life.

## Surround Yourself with Energy

Have you ever reached a time in your life when you stopped yourself progressing on a quest or a goal? Don't fret, you certainly aren't alone. There are many reasons why people will stop on a quest or progress. Too Hard, Too hot, Too heavy. Self-doubt. Criticisms from others. Concern what others will think. Failures and struggles. How many times?

We are blessed with multiple examples where many successes from people, have come directly after failure. Many success stories speak of constant struggles prior to achievement. Stories of self-doubt being over-ridden by a positive mindset are the stuff of legends, while others were rejected and criticised but kept plugging away ultimately to success.

Examples of how success has been achieved by over-coming struggles, failures, self-doubt and put-down are many. However, this is outweighed in sheer number of people who chose to quit or who drop off from their goals.

It's like a beautiful view which you want to explore, but can't because you are fenced in. Don't allow yourself to be fenced in! Don't allow yourself to stop on your quest! Don't let, fear, failure, self-doubt or struggle fence you in. Do not allow it. Like everything, just when you feel you cannot get back up, believe that you are closer to achieving it...because you are. So GET BACK UP! Believe and achieve. You don't know how close you are...don't allow yourself to believe otherwise.

We need more people in this world, energised by chasing a quest or a goal and that is what will energise the world.

WHY NOT MAKE IT YOU!

**STRONGER BRAVER WISER**

# The 3C's –
## Certainty, Comfort, Complacency

Human are creatures of habit. We have heard that for years, but I'm here to tell you that additionally, humans are creatures of comfort. And this leads us to my teaching of the 3C's.

Firstly, we CRAVE CERTAINTY. We love knowing what will/is happening. Generally, we love routine. We get into habits, good and bad. We travel the same routes on the way to work, our work routine rarely changes...our home life becomes a big pile of sameness.

Certainty is what we crave. When we fall outside of our certainty, our reactions are almost immediate. We feel anxious, we feel stressed, we feel UNCOMFORTABLE. So we stick with what is certain. We feel safe.

There is a small group of people that live outside the world of certainty. Some of these operate outside of the law, where the threat of multiple tangibles, not the least getting caught, exist. However even they operate within a level of certainty as planning amongst thieves and criminals usually would be of the calibre that exist in senior business executive. They attempt to minimize the risk or uncertainty. The other group are the adrenalin junkies, who operate in a world in which most of us don't. Their life is about risk, but even they take precautionary stances to minimise the risk.

So generally we CRAVE CERTAINTY. A favourite question comes from Robert H Schuller.

"What would you attempt, if you could not fail"

Every one of us, would be more; we would attempt more if the world existed under these conditions. However, it doesn't. Failure is always one of the big possibilities. So we retreat. And we don't attempt. UNCERTAINTY stops us in our tracks.

In our worlds, we love being spectators. We love peering into the world of uncertainty. We get immersed in movies, we love our sports live, and once we know the scores to a game, we struggle then to watch it. We watch reality TV. Once done, however, we slip right back into our own lives of certainty.

So, I'm not suggesting that we become thieves, or adrenalin junkies. And some habits are good. Just ensure that the certainty in your life, or your routine is enabling you to grow and flourish. That your habits are enlarging you as a person and making you better than yesterday. John Maxwell's Law of Process is all about good daily habits that allow you to grow a little each day, which leads to a massive improvement over the course of a period of time.

But in most cases, our certainty, dulls us and doesn't stoke the embers of that fire that used to burn within...We are heading down the wrong track. You see when we CRAVE CERTAINTY, WE CREATE COMFORT.

When we CRAVE CERTAINTY, WE CREATE COMFORT. Comfort is the enemy of growth, desire and motivation.

We all know couples who have gotten comfortable in their relationship; they put on weight, they stop trying for each other and themselves. They get comfortable.

We get comfortable in our jobs; we learn what we need to do to stay out of trouble. The stretch, the challenge that was there just goes. And we get caught in the mundane. We aim for average.

We choose to fly under the radar.

Comfort is different things to different people. The threat and stress of change, cannot compete with comfort. We get confused when we see people who stay in destructive relationships, we see couples that stay together for the kids, even though they have grown apart; these people have found a level of comfort in their situation, it's what they know. And change is more frightening. They get comfortable.

Growth and learning occurs outside of our comfort zone. For most we are firmly entrenched within.

Abraham Maslow said "we step forward to growth, or step backwards to safety". Sadly, most will step back. The fear of the new, overwhelms us and we retreat to comfort.

So by CRAVING CERTAINTY, WE CREATE COMFORT.

We Crave Certainty, we Create Comfort and ultimately Cause Complacency.

Because when we get comfortable, we get lazy. We take shortcuts, we don't take due care. We operate as automatic drones as we endure life. In effect, we stop living, we just haven't made it official.

The world today mass produces average. We talk about things needing to change, sadly it's all talk. Or we talk about others needing to change, and neglect the fact the only person we can change is ourselves.

Life should be enjoyed. Our lives are what we create. When we become a creature of comfort, we face the 3C's. We accept what life brings, and in doing so we minimise life itself

Everything is not lost. You can have certainty and routine and growth. Ensure your habits involve a process where you are challenged. Doing some simple things daily will help. Reading, Learning, Conversing are great habits to get into.

Our routines should enable us to grow and flourish and our habits should enlarge us and make us better than yesterday. Good daily habits allow us to grow a little each day, and will lead to a massive improvement over time. This challenge to grow requires courage to continually change or improve ourselves. BUT It is our own personal evolution.

So, the 3C's can be broken by using another 3C's.That of Challenge, Courage and Change.

Remember life is an occasion, we simply must rise to it.

## Simply Musing – I Went Surfing Today

I went surfing this morning. Like everyone, I have had some tough times in my life and surfing has always been a solace for me. Time to hang the feet over the side of the board, sit, reflect, rely on instinct to catch some waves and enjoy some ME time.

It's fair to say, that this time has also kept me going during those rough spots that come up in life. Instinct and living in the now are the things that allow me to get focus, and get away from any problems. Peering over the edge of a peeling four-foot left hander, is not the time to think about anything. Jumping to my feet and surfing that way is instinct and nothing else matters. The solace of the surfer.

There I was this morning, at my favourite spot at Tugan on the Gold Coast. Itching to get into the water, as I have been busy laying down plans for an amazing year. The time on the water, again had the same process as before. Instead of my mind whirling through all the plans, excitement, travel and new business ventures that I'm facing up to, the water again had a calming effect as I plonked the feet over the side of the board, sat, reflected and used my instinct to catch a few waves and have some fun.

I lived the now, lived the present moment and took some time out and that is how I go forward.

"There is a big difference between losing and seeing yourself as a loser. Everyone who has had success has suffered a loss or losses at many stages, they have just kept going until they succeed. We choose how we react when we lose. Excuses and entitlement are two of our greatest challenges in the world."

"If you settle for simply existing, you miss the chance of exhilaration."

"We are masters of self-deceit. We listen to our excuses. Stop being a slave to your lies."

*"What legacy we leave will be determined by what we do daily. Are you intentional in what you do, are you aware of the role you have in guiding those close to you? Yes, a legacy will be left by you, but it's your actions that determine how positive it will be."*

*"Internal questions, internal blocks, internal lies... The things that stop most of us are internal. We stop ourselves before we can complete what it is we are meant to do."*

*"Today should be top of the pops. Stop replaying the soundtrack of yesterday, update, modernise, focus on today."*

"Having a great attitude is a choice. And what a choice. People with great attitudes are great to be around. People with great attitudes have greater success. What is your attitude doing for you?"

"You could achieve everything if it wasn't for the buts! Stop listening to your buts."

"It's one thing to try and not succeed. It's another not to try and never know."

# Getting Out of Butville – Making YOU the Priority

A former colleague of mine, "Rabbit", made an art-form of saying "YEAAAA, BUT. It was an ongoing inside joke. Whenever with ideas, thoughts or brainstorms that didn't make the grade, Rabbit would go into an exaggerated YYYYEEEEEEEEAAAAAAAAA, BUT. We'd have a laugh and get on with it.

But it's not a joke when people are ruled by the "Yea-But". Just as many may be, as they read through self-help books (maybe even this one), the BUTS that rule in our lives.

- I'd love to start a business, BUT....
- I'd love to write a book, BUT....
- I'd love to record a song, BUT...
- I should leave my partner, BUT....

As I have heard said so many times, you're living in Butville, the land where your buts rule your life. That one simple word that stops us in our tracks. It kills any positive feeling that the previous words portray, much like Rabbit, we use it ourselves to kill off any further progression of the idea being expressed.

And that's so sad.

In our graveyards there are songs, books, thoughts and creative works of art that will be forever unpublished, unrecorded, unappreciated. Buried forever.

Seriously, what will it take to realise the gifts you have and what gives you the right not to share them with the world. I love the fact that I can write and impact people sharing my thoughts and idea easily and quickly.

When I start coaching people, we discover simple blocks very early on. Whether it's self-limiting beliefs, or blocks caused by living in Butville, we commence a process that break them down to get forward traction.

You see, many people provide advice, share words and make people feel better. People get goose-bumps, shed tears, become vulnerable, make vows and promises and still get nowhere.

We don't get action and therefore don't get traction.

We don't make ourselves the priority to make the leap of faith. But it can be done. Let me share how I made my purpose a priority.

**Purpose**

Purpose. Another word being overused. We are told to find our purpose and we create our life. We hear it, we read it. Our purpose, this magical thing that lifts us higher than anything else can. And it can. It just seems that no-one really tells us how to do that.

Simply, it's use hasn't enabled mass change in mentality. In fact, it has probably achieved more mass cynicism. Why? Because knowing you have a purpose isn't enough. You have to know how to achieve it, you need more than just having one.

So we struggle. We struggle because of our current commitments; our current circumstances. They don't allow us the time to reflect, let alone to dream and, heaven forbid, finding the time to achieve your purpose.

Our current priorities: our current commitments: our current jobs: our current circumstances.

And you talk about purpose? How about keeping food on the table, a roof over my head and the ability to pay the bills? That's life and my purpose will just have to wait. That's my reality, having a purpose is really just a dream.

I understand that. Amazingly well. 30 years' experience of that exact mindset gives me that understanding. But I escaped and you can too. And you should! It's a case of making your purpose a priority. Let me share my way forward.

**Priorities**

I use a leadership concept from John Maxwell to help me prioritise my day. I use the 3R's. Do what's required, do what gives you best return and finally do what rewards you. Using that as a base, I built a process which has enable me to progress towards my purpose and added two steps of my own.

1.  Do what's REQUIRED. This takes two parts for people looking for purpose. Do what is required to honour your current commitments. Hold that job, do what's necessary to keep food on the table and a roof over your head. You cannot achieve your purpose, your dream when you're starving on the streets. BUT, you also need discipline to take steps daily to achieve your dreams. Define those steps and take them; every day. If you want to be a writer, WRITE. If you want to be a speaker, SPEAK. *It is that simple.*

137

Do what's necessary every day, and by doing so you get closer to your dream every day.

2. Do what gets you the greatest return. What opportunities exist for you? Are you even looking? What can you be doing to get you the return needed to start working more on your purpose?

3. Do what gives you greatest reward. When people work on their purpose and their passion, it shows in their satisfaction levels. When what you do, gives you great reward, great return AND is what's required, then you are truly working on your purpose. You know it, you feel it. You're immersed in it.

4. Review your results. By adding a review step, you can check your progress and add reality into the mix. Reviewing isn't meant as a sign for you to bash yourself up either. NO WAY, it's to give you an appreciation of your progress. By placing a priority on your purpose, you take daily steps and you get closer to your dream. Recognise it, reward yourself and keep it up.

5. Refresh. Simply it's needed. Take time to refresh to ensure that your dream is really your dream. Refresh and get moving again.

## Progress

Don't accept your current reality as a reason not to chase your dreams. On your deathbed, you won't be lying there wishing you had given more to that 9 to 5 job, that bad relationship, or whatever it is constraining you now. No, you will be wishing you had pursued your dreams, your goals, your greatest desire. You will be wishing that you had fulfilled your purpose. You can do this, by making your purpose a priority..

Follow these five steps make your purpose a priority. Get started. When you find yourself in that wonderful position where what you are doing is required, provides return, gives you reward, you're getting results and it refreshes you.....you are in the zone, you have found your purpose. That's the aim, that's the goal,

You've got this.

## Simply, It's Time

The world you live in is evolving and progressing at a faster rate than ever experienced in history. In a world governed by marketing and the latest thing, the rate of despair and unhappiness amongst our people is also rising at a faster rate.

You may feel unmotivated. You may feel stuck. You may feel that life isn't so great. You may feel that the best has left you behind. You may be disengaged.

You may feel that you have failed. Success wasn't meant for you. Your circumstances are what is governing your progress in the world, governing how you identify with the world, and ultimately how the world communicate with you.

Life is hard, and getting harder every day.

You are stuck. Stuck in a routine, stuck in a relationship, you cannot move.

You are stuck.

And you have done some things to help. You researched the "magic pill". You joined the social media groups and share how you feel. But all you feel is even more angst as others seem to be getting their shit together yet you haven't seen any transformation.

It just makes you feel worse.

You may have a vision board, you may meditate, you may have set your intentions.

Yet
Nothing is happening.

You paid out a lot of money on an online course, but after a couple of lessons you dropped it as it wasn't changing anything.

You've listened to the GURUS. You have waited long enough.

And you are ready to hear some news. Something new. Something simple.

And here it is.
THERE IS NO MAGIC PILL FOR ANY OF THIS. NONE THAT CAN BE GIVEN TO YOU OR PROVIDED TO YOU OR BOUGHT FOR YOU.

The MAGIC PILL, lies in you. It sits within the very fabric of who you are, what you are made of. All the successes and wins from your ancestry are within you now. The magic is there. And you have waited long enough to unleash it to the world.

Your greatest potential is within reach. It lies within eye-sight. It's within arm reach. It's time.

Simply, It's time.

**STRONGER BRAVER WISER**

## Simple Strategy Time

You've read the book and learnt some new things and now you are ready to have a real go at breaking the feeling of being stuck. The Magic formula is YOU. So let's look at what YOU can do. These four simple questions will take you a long way. Get out there, let's get it done!

| 1.  What do you want? |
| --- |
| |

| 2. Can you describe it in less than 25 words? |
| --- |
| |

| 3. What is the very next step you can take? What do you have to do every day to keep that forward motion? |
| --- |
| |

**4. How do you keep this in front of you? How do you keep it clear?**

## Seriously

*"Simply said, you can be more. You may be wondering around life in a struggle to get ahead, you may have stopped trying or attempting to excel, you may even be asking yourself "What's the Point" the point is this. Your life of greater significance and satisfaction is waiting there for you and is found within you..... It's within you now, you just have to unearth it. You can do that, take time daily with yourself, no distractions, just you and your breathing. Do this daily and you will uncover what you have been hiding all this time."*

*"Seriously, it's all about the journey. How we live is how we feel about success. Let your story uplift others, let your journey inspire you."*

"Seriously, why put energy into excuses? Why? Channel your energy into intentional action. Dedicate energy into driving your very best version of you. Stop the excuses, stop that mentality. Channel the best version of you."

"Simply Musing. Stop apologising. to yourself, to others. Everything you need is within you right now. Stop apologising and simply get moving. Move towards your greatest self."

"Seriously, just stop. Appreciate everything that is around you."

*"Seriously special. Seriously YOU!"*

*"The time is right. The time is now. Reach up and grab hold of the life that you want. It's yours. Unass the couch, take the steps you need. You've got this."*

*"Seriously, everytime we miss an opportunity to unite, all we do is strengthen the divide."*

## Carter's Cause

Thank you for the purchase of this book. Part of the proceeds of your purchase goes towards Carter's Cause a Brisbane Not-for-Profit raising funds and awareness for children born with Cognitive Heart Disease.

Jarade and Ashleigh McFillin were expecting their first child in May of 2013. Everyone was ecstatic as this was to be the 5th grandchild of our very dear friends, Stuart and Carol, of over 20 years. We had seen Ashleigh grow into a beautiful young women and had known Jarade since he was 18. It was during our yearly January camping holiday with all the families, that we had been doing for a number of years, that Jarade and Ashleigh had to return to Brisbane for a 20-week scan. They returned with some news that would eventually turn their world upside down. Their baby had a heart condition. It was plumbed backwards.

What was to happen in the following months you would not wish on anyone. The rollercoaster of emotions that Ashleigh and Jarade would go through were more than anybody should have to bare.

Baby Carter Desmond McFillin was born 5 weeks and 1 day early, on the 26th of April 2013, and would require heart surgery to have a chance at life.

During his short life, Carter developed many complications, that stopped the heart surgery from going ahead.

Although he fought so bravely through all of this, he was unable to have that heart surgery and sadly, passed away on the 26th of May 2013.

Thinking about the babies and children going through this day after day. Thinking about the parents of those children with heart disease or heart conditions that may have to come from a rural or remote town, having to uplift their lives and come to an unfamiliar place while their child was in hospital getting all of the possible medical support they could.

I felt that I could do something to help those babies or those parents and, hopefully, make life a little easier for them. Most of all I wanted to show Ashleigh and Jarade that even though my family had never experienced a loss like this, I still felt their pain and wanted to do something to help.

Again, I thank you for purchasing this book and helping our cause. If you wish to help in any other way, please contact me. The children and the families thank you.

Sharon Curl – President
Carter's Cause
president@carterscause.org.au
**www.carterscause.org.au**

# About Tony Curl

Tony is an Empowerment Coach, and was the first coach in Australia certified in Psycho-Neuro-Actualization, the ground-breaking and effective coaching and influencing tool developed by Dr. Steve Maraboli. He is currently undertaking further studies in the field. He works with clients to align their actions with the desires of their greatest potential. He helps decode those bad habits and behaviours that keep people stuck, de-activates them and allows them to shine. He shares his #dailyfuel picture quotes and messages on his growing social media platforms, helping people to #breaktheshackles of self-limitations.

Tony has been a successful corporate leader for 30 years. He now works alongside leaders around the world, and at home in Australia, to maintain clarity on their vision and purpose, and helps map their way around their roadblocks and obstacles. Tony helps people take the steps in their lives to become an influential leader. The leaders Tony helps aspire to greatness, so if you are aspiring to greatness take steps today. Unless you take action on your goals, they remain a dream.

He is published at A Better Today Media, A Better Today Australia, Simple Reminders Network, Realizing Leadership, Ezine, Leadership Inspiration and on his own clog site CoachCurl.com

Coach Curl has a range of services that can help you get UNSTUCK. Tony and his wife Sharon are the only two certified coaches in Australia on the "Maraboli Method", Psycho-Neuro-Actualization and they can help you achieve your greatest self, your greatest version of you, your greatest potential.

It's time to wake up, it's time to stand up for you. Let's get UNSTUCK. Let's Break the Shackles of your Self-Limitations. Let's launch to your greatest desires.

**Break the Shackles**

Are you stuck? Are you waiting for better? Are you wanting better? Something is holding you back. Break your Shackles of Self-Doubt in just four weeks.

Do you wake up believing you are capable of more but unsure how to realise this capability? do you have a goal but lack clarity as to how to achieve it?

"Breaking the Shackles" is a program that works and will work for YOU. It is a four-week coaching program that sees you take the first steps towards your greater potential. This four-week period is all you need to have clarity on your achievement and potential.

**The Four Pillars of Success**

Losing the battle with the outdated version of you? The Four Pillars of Success is a SIMPLE method of attaining the life you desire.

And we guarantee it!!

SICK OF SELF-SABOTAGE?

Stop SHADOW-BOXING with the OUT-DATED version of you!

Keeping promises to yourself is hard, using the information we possess to build the life of our dreams is hard, aligning our actions to our goals is hard.

If you are sick of WAITING, tired of your excuses then register today for the FOUR PILLARS OF SUCCESS workshop and have all the tools you will ever need.

**Mindset Shift Mentoring**

Activate and maintain a shift in your mindset.

Experience tells us that people fall short of achieving sustainable positive change in their life due to an inability to shift mindset to accommodate the new habits and behaviours needed for positive change.

Everyone has two competing people within themselves. They have their best version of themselves, filled with great intention and belief, and they have an outdated version of themselves, wishing for nothing but more of the same.

Undoubtedly Tony will help you rise above to become the greatest version of yourself. Stop waiting, start your journey today, the journey that drives a new reality from what is possible for you.

Contact him today to help you get moving towards the life your absolutely deserve.

Tony Curl – tonycurl.com
P: 1300 866 928
Int.P: +61 417 197 149
E: tony@tonycurl.com

**Testimonials**

### Catherine B. Roy

*"I met Tony at The Royal Society. He is very creative professional and extremely intelligent person who develops incredible synergy with everyone who is given the opportunity to work with him! He is a mission oriented leader and mentor with exceptional leadership skills. I highly recommend Tony as high level professional Business Coach."*

### Nicholas Smith

*"I learnt more about leadership during Tony's 6-week leadership course, then I did during 7-years with the army. Tony's knowledge on the subject of leadership is just remarkable, and I highly recommend him to anyone who want's to improve their leadership skills, whether for business or personal. Thanks Tony, and I look forward to future courses!"*

### Brad Tupper

*"The process, people and content of this course was absolutely outstanding. I can honestly say it exceeded my expectations by far, and Tony and Wendy are two of the nicest, humblest people you*

*could ever wish to meet, with a wealth of their own life experience to top it all off. Do yourself a favour and don't hesitate, these two wonderful people are genuine in their approach, delivery and all round kind nature. A great couple of weeks!"*

### Laura and Gavin Armstrong

*"Tony, I wanted you to know that your workshop had such a positive & powerful influence on our lives and I would highly recommend couples like us doing it together particularly. Thank you again for your role in our amazing year of ticking off goals big & small!"*

### Franz Braun

*"Everything rises and falls on leadership" and Tony can help you succeed in your business with your most important Assets with is you / your staff or career through his coaching. Have used Tony's Services not only to further my knowledge, but it helped me and my team to understand the different aspects of Leadership. I found the way he delivered the knowledge was not only very beneficial for all but he encouraged all of us ."*

**Kylie Fiebig**

*"Thank you for an amazing week, Tony! You're inspirational, I really appreciated the opportunity to learn from you."*

**Cindy Anelante · New York University**

*Thank you Tony Curl for the excellent article. Your wisdom resonates with me. It just takes a little time and effort to organize our lives to a simpler albeit not simplistic way of being and living. For me, your points on clarity are spot on! I take notes on my iPad, in a notebook and also on post its which I place on a couple of places at home as reminders toward clarity and the wishes I have for my life. I truly appreciate your thoughts. Simple, pure, living is a beautiful way of being. It is a Royal way of life!*

**Denise Joline Nehila · Photographer at Denise Nehila Photography**

*"Don't wait another day waiting for someday or one day." This is my favorite line and speaks volumes. One day those some days will be gone and then it will be too late. Thanks for the great article.*

**Melissa Rose Rothschild · Life coach, Author, Inspirational Speaker, Philanthropist at Princess Rothschild Crowned**

*Simple, not easy, but worth it! Thank you for sharing.*

**Danette Mark · Works at Stand Up Comedian**

*Doing is key! And, yes we fail to DO things at times. Great Message!!*

**Dawn Odegard ·**

*Thank you for this wonderful article. Simplifying and gaining focus where needed, and letting go of what is not needed or is hurting us in some way. All these choices of focus lead to clarity, which leads to peace, serenity and growth. Again, thank you for sharing. Very helpful.*

**Erin Taylor · Contributing Writer/Blogger at SRN.net**

*Thank you, Tony. Simplify and purify. I love those two words together!*

**Shelly Watson · Maryville University**

*Fantastic article. Alignment is the key. Tapping into the energy of what you want and taking action. Thank you for the reminder*

***Sandra Schell Geiss · Owner-operator at SilverSchells***

*Thank you Tony Curl I am going take this and make a clear action plan. Exciting!*

***Kay Stern***

*Wow Tony Curl. What a great read. Your thoughts are mine. I loved your article and so true. Simplicity and purity and authenticity is the best way to go. Thanks for this powerful tool!*

***Dorothy McDermott · CEO at Me, Myself and I Corp.***

*you are a great inspiration struggling with life is no fun if you find a little help it goes a long way to betterment of the soul thanks*

***Sherie Lynn Sixkiller-Wing · Kingman, Arizona***

*Thank you!!! Awesome direction!!! Read ponder apply!*

***Bonnie Bono · Creative Writer at Bonnie Cochrane***

*Wow!! This is a fantastic read!! Thank you so much for sharing this article Tony! What you say here deeply resonates with me.*

### Jannette Hoeksema · Noorderpoort College Groningen

*Very clear message and steps to follow in our actions. Really helpfull, thank you for sharing Sir Tony.*

### Sarah M Capehart

*Amazing, thank you!! "We fall in love with our original plan when we should fall in love with the goal." Simply amazing, Tony. I loved everything about this article. Thanks for the Simple Reminder, one I desperately needed to here. Looking forward to much more from you!*

### Maria Koszler · Creative Writer at MTK Publications

*A beautiful article, thank you for sharing*

### Angela Bush

*Thought provoking article Tony. Thank you for pointing out the importance of silence and stillness.*

### Marleen Lundy - BRM Institute

*Thank you for coming out to close our event. You did a great job and your story is fascinating. I know our attendees gained valuable insight from both of your presentations.*

### Bronwyn Ritchie - Pivotal Points Consulting

*"Tony's presentation was totally engaging, progressed organically and presented information that was relevant and memorable."*

### Alice Langford. Manager Business Enterprise Centre Brisbane Metro

*Some of the leadership lessons you provided within the talk, particularly resonated with many and they went away from the breakfast event with a new awareness and plans for action. What was most inspiring was your down to earth approach and ability to connect with the new business owners and how they listened sincerely to every word you said.*

### Angela Stafford - Angela's Wild Kitchen

*Tony is a very warm and approachable teacher and coach. His ideas are inspiring and he is able to break long term goals down into smaller, achievable steps. I found that having Tony as a teacher enabled me to look at my business in more practical terms and gave me a clearer vision of where I want to take it.*

**Starla Borges - Business Relationship Management Institute**

*I wanted to send a quick note of congratulations on your sessions at our conference. While I was not there, I have been receiving live feedback throughout the day, and the reviews have been phenomenal. I'm so glad that we discovered you, you have been a welcome addition to our conference. Thank you so much, and hoping we can work together again one day.*

**Adrian De La Cruz ,Australian Made Product Evangelist ♦ Founder at Tixxy Pty Ltd**

*It was mid 2013 when Tony and I met at Toastmaster Capalaba for a leadership and public speaking experience. I also learned about his Think and Grow Business at that time. During those meetings, Tony displays his passion for leadership. So when I decided to start my business I asked him to help me out. With his extensive knowledge in business and leadership, he was able to guide me in setting my actionable plans. Tony was also the business mentor to the successful Building a Better Business Mentoring Program where he coached a group of small business owners, myself included, on*

163

*how to create an effective business action plan, how to stay relevant in the current business environment, and how to be mentally and emotionally resilient when conducting business. Tony displayed exemplary listening skill which help him tailor solutions to unique businesses. If you are starting out or planning to scale up your business, Tony can help you make a framework of effective strategies which will save you time and spare you from headaches. Clarity is your friend. I highly recommend Tony Curl*

### Bruce Nicholls, Health and Safety Professional

*"I have known Tony for a number of years. Initially he supported me in my journey of physical transformation for which I am grateful. I have also worked alongside Tony as mentors for people chasing positive change and physical transformation in their lives. He is an inspiring and energetic person who truly lives what he teaches. I have seen him work with people to achieve their goals and have personally seen how transforming his presentations and workshops can be. All up, he remains a "good bloke" and authentic and one of his great qualities is that he doesn't take himself too seriously" He love what he does and it shows in the care he has for others. I have no hesitation in recommending Tony*

*to anyone chasing goals and transformation in their lives*

**Clare O'Donohue, Events and Marketing Professional.**

*"Thank you, Tony! It was a great session-definitely one of the best and most reflective events I have ever been to. The actionable outcomes, of course, are a huge take-away from the session.*

**STRONGER BRAVER WISER**

www.strongerbraverwiser.com

**The CoachCurl Network**

www.coachcurl.com

www.abettertoday.com.au

www.thinkandgrowbusiness.com.au

www.strongerbraverwiser.com.au

# *20% of EVERY SALE goes to Carter's Cause*

*Thank you for your support.*

CPSIA information can be obtained
at www.ICGtesting.com
Printed in the USA
BVOW04s0237131216
470625BV00018B/307/P